## EXCERPT FROM CHAPTER 1

The coming chapters will bring stories of multiple raging storms ranging from divorce, death of a first-born child and grandson, a son serving in the Iraq war, a daughter in drugs and sexual immortality who eventually took my grandchildren from me and entered witchcraft, terminal illness, death of my ex-husband and death of my second husband, spiritual abuse by various churches and pastors, and finally the sexual molestation and impregnation of my minor daughter by a Christian pastor/counselor. These may seem like unbearable trials brought on back to back, but these chapters will also bring stories of incredible miracles, signs, and wonders (visits to heaven), redemption, salvation, comfort, healing, forgiveness, hope, and love!

At the forefront of this book I would like to challenge all who read this book to see God as exceedingly and abundantly above all one can think or ask (Ephesians 3:20). He is great and powerful and works all things for the good of those who love Him (Romans 8:28). He (Jesus) is the mighty right hand of God.

I would like to thank my husband, children, and each individual that encouraged me in this endeavor – you know who you are. I would also like to thank all my brothers and sisters in Christ who were obedient to the voice of God to tell me to write this book and had the faith to believe I could accomplish it.

**This book is based on a true story, but names and personal or private details of events have been changed or omitted for the protection of all individuals involved.**

# Table of Contents

**FORWARD** .................................................................................... 5

**PREFACE** ...................................................................................... 11

**CHAPTER I**
Salvation and Deliverance
..................................................................................... 17

**CHAPTER II**
Cyclone Divorce and Death
..................................................................................... 38

**CHAPTER III**
Miracles in the Fiery Furnace
..................................................................................... 70

**CHAPTER IV**
Amazing Grace
..................................................................................... 90

**CHAPTER V**
The Aftermath: Drugs, Sex, and War
..................................................................................... 138

**CHAPTER VI**
Witchcraft (Yikes)
..................................................................................... 155

## CHAPTER VII
Winds of Sickness, Depression, & Spiritual Abuse
...................................................................................................... 165

## CHAPTER VIII
Storms of Leukemia & Death
..................................................................................................... 194

## CHAPTER IX
Hurricane Christian Counselor:
Betrayal of Authority & Broken Trust
..................................................................................................... 222

## CHAPTER X
Angels Present & Heavenly Encounters
..................................................................................................... 233

# FORWARD

Time was nearing the end! "The light at the end of the tunnel" as the old saying goes. Five years of excruciatingly hard work on a journey toward a Bachelor's Degree in Health Psychology while crises crashed into my life like lightning showers out of the sky. The instruction God had given me several years earlier, "Go to college," I could not begin to understand. Blind obedience was what I was trying to accomplish. Several individuals over the last year have spoken with me about my life. After hearing some of the stories, time and again it has been said to me, "You need to write a book!" Friends, strangers, acquaintances, fellow workers, it did not seem to matter; I continued to hear the same comment. Strangely enough, this seemed a repeat of fourteen years earlier when I wrote my first book. God used various individuals during the week of planning my daughter and grandson's funeral to tell me to "write a book." I did that very thing; I had it put into print but never felt the "heart-tug" to have it published. I bought about seven hundred copies and either sold or gave them as a gift. I was astounded by how many people called me crying and wanted to share stories about how the Lord had used the book for physical, emotional, mental or spiritual healing of wounds that were thought could never be healed.  I was humbled by the Lord's sovereign hand and great power.  So, here I sit again wondering how God can use my life story and another book to encourage, uplift, uphold, heal, educate, and possibly even astound individuals.

God started using people in the early part of 2014 to confirm His will in my life.  During my fourth to last class before graduation another tragedy hit my life.  I was getting weary and sadness was overwhelming me.  On my way to class one Monday night, I asked the Lord to confirm to me that I was to write another book.  I was scared, overwhelmed, overworked, and there was no time for myself.  I remember questioning God about what He could possibly want out of another book.  "Was this tragic life of mine important enough for someone to glean anything valuable or for God to be able to glorify Himself?"  This question seemed to haunt me as the words "You need to write a book!" came over and over again in my head.  God got right on the job and swiftly answered my question.  After class the professor asked me how my daughter and husband were.  Tears welled up in my eyes as I told him another tragic story.  He was shocked and commented on my strength and joy even in overwhelming circumstances. I quickly declared it was the grace of God and His strength because without Him, I could never endure such troubles and tribulations. As we were walking out of class and saying our goodbyes, we turned our backs on one another to walk in opposite directions. He stopped, turned, and stated, "Lily, you need to write a book!" I was stunned and stammered out the question, "Why would you say that?" He immediately responded telling me that he felt the Lord prompt him to tell me this. I guess this final confirmation is why I am sitting here trying to put into words fifty-one years of trials, tribulations, and tragedies filled with grace, mercy, hope, and miracles. Amazingly enough, I had the same professor for my second to last class; at the end of the final class he smiled at me and told me that he was astounded by the grace of God and the miracles that God was working in my life. Then he nodded at me and said, "When you finish that book let me know and I will arrange a book signing in the town where I live." Tears stung my eyes and threatened to hit the ground as I commented, "I'll hold you to that word, it's a deal." Now, graduation is December 2014, and even though my husband's body will not be present, I know he will be smiling from heaven as proud as any man could be. "I did it!" I accomplished one of the most difficult tasks of my life – five years of college amongst some of the most horrific, tragic, and difficult events that any family would want to live through. Now I am working on the accomplishment of another difficult task – this book. I am unsure, hesitant, scared, and many other adjectives I could add, as I contemplate this book. When I think I have missed the mark or couldn't possibly have anything to offer the reader, God will find another way to give me a little push. Two examples: I work at an Assisted Living/Memory Care, and I was out planning an outing for the residents. I stopped by the Senior Citizen Center to find out about the Music Jam that was playing that week and while speaking with the Director of the establishment I ended up sharing a little about my husband's walk through Leukemia. She was astounded and at the end of our conversation she looked at me and stated, (you guessed right) "You need to write a book!" I chuckled and told her that I had begun this task. She smiled and informed me that the book would be an amazing story that would astound readers and help guide them through various trials. Second example: In December 2014, I had an entertainer come to the establishment where I work to do a Christmas event. I hired this young woman a few times because she is an amazing performer. We became friends through the course of the last three years. She asked me how life had been, and I shared about the death of my husband and how difficult yet wonderful the last eight months had been. I had shared with her earlier that year that I was going to write a book and after we talked for about thirty minutes she told me that she knew people and would arrange for a book signing and a radio interview. She told me that she had never heard such amazing stories and told me I needed to share with others so that they could glean from my life. I was humbled at this offer. This may seem redundant and even ridiculous that God would use so many people to nudge me forward, but here I am writing my life story not only for enjoyment of reading but hopefully help through trials and troubles as well as to see that God loves you greatly and cares about every small and large circumstance in your life. He wants to help, guide, comfort, and glorify Himself through the pain and rejoicing of your life. I pray that He will use these stories to help break the hold of the enemy in your life and bring love, hope, joy, and peace that are beyond what can even be understood.

After hours of thought and prayer I came up with what I decided was the Lord's instruction on what I was to do and what kind of book I was to write. With the first book, God had instructed me to write the book as if I was sitting down and having tea with an individual and sharing our family's story, so that is what I intend to do. This book will be a trilogy of three separate time periods that are to be combined into one incredible story. I will include the first book: *Though He Slay Me, Yet Shall I Praise Him* (Job 13:15); a second manuscript: *Out of the Miry Clay, I Have Set Your Feet upon a Rock* (Psalm 40:1-3); and the third and final portion will conclude the trilogy with a story based around the verse that was given to my husband when he was diagnosed with Leukemia. He had asked the Lord to tell him what was to happen to him and how he was to walk through Leukemia. This was the answer: "Blessed is the man whose strength is in You, Whose heart is set on pilgrimage. As they pass through the Valley of Baca. They make it a spring; the rain also covers it with pools. They go from strength to strength; each one appears before God in Zion" (Psalm 84:5-7). At this time, I invite you to grab that cup of tea or coffee and lounge back for an amazing, shocking, and glorifying to God story.

# PREFACE

I believe it was my eleventh birthday; I opened the gift of a lifetime. Though it was inexpensive, I treasured it above every other thing I owned. It was a "Big Chief" bright red writing pad. I was thrilled over such a simple gift. I had asked Mom for it because I wanted to write poetry and short stories and oh, what a passion I had for that. Then it happened; I wrote my first short story. It was a two-hundred thirty page, hand-written love story (pretty impressive for a little girl of eleven years old, huh?). A very crude attempt at a love story to say the least, but it was all mine. Then came the day of my ultimate devastation - my sister took my story without permission and read it. Not only that, then she critiqued it with red marker where she made very bad remarks about it. These remarks damaged my heart greatly causing me to march out to the garbage barrel and incinerate my precious story. As I ripped the story to shreds and struck the match to light it on fire, I looked up to heaven sobbing and declared to God that I would NEVER write another thing as long as I lived. Little did I know that twenty-six years later the Lord would make that "never" come true!

A short while before my daughter and grandson's death (which I thought was the most devastating tragedy a mother could endure) I was reading a book called *Yaffa, God's Prickly Pear*. It was at the beginning of me reading this book that the Lord spoke to my heart and said, "I want **you** to write a book." To say the least, I laughed out loud and told God that I could not write a book. I could not imagine what I would possibly write about in a book. When I finished the last chapter of the book I was reading, God again spoke to me and told me that He wanted me to write a book. My answer: "Lord, I do not know how to do this and I cannot." It was not long after speaking this word to me, that God started sending individuals my way to confirm what He had asked me to do. Of all days to start this journey, the Lord used the day that my sister, my daughter, and I were sitting at the table making poster boards for the funeral to speak to me about when I was a young girl and what happened with my love story. While we were talking, I started to relay the story of what happened when I was a little girl. I spoke of the "Big Chief" tablet and the devastation of the story. I started sobbing uncontrollably and felt the Lord remove all the pain of what happened to me as a little girl that fateful day. It shocked my sister and daughter that I was crying so hard about what they thought was a silly incident. They did not understand that it was the Lord's way of preparing me for a painful yet healing journey of writing my life story. After I stopped crying, the Lord gently spoke to my heart and said, "Now, you can write that book." He had me convinced, but He needed to give me the "push" to sit at a computer and start. The Lord ended up using my daughter and grandson's wake as a spring-board to finally push me into this task. It was here that a lady came up to me and said, "You need to write a book." Again, the only thought I can remember having: "What can I possibly write about in a book?" The Lord quietly spoke to my heart about how He wanted me to write a book to help individuals heal through pain by forgiveness and love.

As I pondered the task of writing this book, God continued to use individuals to confirm to me that this was His will in my life. I was taking a tambourine class at a nearby church and the teacher had become a friend of mine. She called me that week and told me that she had been sick the whole week. I thought she called me for prayer but that was not it at all. She told me that while she was very sick that week, she was lying in bed praying for my husband and me. I interrupted her (at the prompting of the Lord) and told her that I had to write a book. How weird it was that I completely changed the subject. This was something that I don't normally do. She was stunned. She got very quiet and then stated that while she was praying that week, God had spoken to her heart and told her that she needed to call me and tell me to write a book. She relayed to me that she was not sure how to do that considering I home-schooled and had seven children left at home. She stated that she knew I did not have time to write and then told God that He needed to open a door in the conversation about writing a book so that she could relay the message to me. That is exactly what He did! He used me to interrupt her conversation to tell her that I had to write a book so that she could confirm this to me.

Wouldn't you think that God would stop right there and that I would just be able to sit down and write a book? Well, He didn't because He needed to convince my husband, Louis. My husband always needed "a brick threw at him" in order for him to relent and allow me to do what God wanted me to do. He was **not** convinced that I was supposed to do such a crazy and expensive endeavor. Shortly after the conversation with my tambourine teacher, Louis and I went to our Tuesday night Life Group meeting from our church.  On the way to the meeting, my husband asked me if I was sure that God wanted me to write a book.  I assured him that God had spoken, and I was to do this.  I asked him to please not make me doubt and to pray for me.  He agreed but told me that I was not to share with anyone that I was to write a book.  I agreed, but while we were at the group, we started sharing the testimonies of what had happened at the funeral of our daughter and grandson.  The Life Group leader listened to all the miraculous and wonderful things God had been doing and stated, "You need to write a book!"  I chuckled as Louis was jolted by God.  We ended up sharing with the group about how God had orchestrated all these events so that we knew beyond a shadow of a doubt that I was to write a book.

One of my prayers for you, the reader, is that by the end of this book you will be able to stand on God's promises through your sorrow and pain. Many individuals, including myself, have stood upon promises inclusive of "Though He slay me, yet shall I trust Him" (Job 13:15) and "I waited patiently for the Lord; and He inclined to me and heard my cry. He brought me up out of the pit of destruction, out of the miry clay; and He set my feet upon a rock making my footsteps firm. He put a new song in my mouth, a song of praise to our God. Many will see and fear, and will trust in the Lord" (Psalm 40:1-3).

# CHAPTER I

# SALVATION AND DELIVERANCE

It was August, 1989, and I was sitting in my bedroom late in the evening contemplating the worst thing anyone could possibly think about. I was deciding on the most painless way I could kill myself. Suicide was it; the only way I could think to get myself out of the extreme depression and loneliness in which I was living. But at that moment a thought popped into my head. If I do this, my three children, who at the time were three, four, and five years old, would have to go live with their father, John, who was an addict of every kind: drug, alcohol, gambling, and pornography. He would surely destroy their lives, and I could not possibly fathom this. In desperation, I cried out to a God that I was sure was not there or had, in the least, abandoned me. How does one get to the lowest point of suicide? This is my story:

I lived in a home that was, to use the "buzz" word, dysfunctional. My father seemed to be angry most of the time and my mother was very controlling. There was yelling, swearing, and abuse of all forms. When I was young, I could remember different instances where there was abuse to my siblings. The funny thing was that it was never done to me. I did not get physically abused in any way. I can remember being yelled and swore at but never physically harmed. Part of the reason was because I believe God protected me and partly, I was extremely afraid of my father. I did not like physical pain at all; because of this, I was a very obedient and compliant child. Even as a teenager, I did everything that was required of me. My siblings weren't quite as compliant as I, so they suffered my father and mother's wrath. "My pain" came from being ignored. You see, my father was very disappointed in me when I was born. He already had three girls, and he wanted a boy really bad. My mother once told me that the doctors had told her and my father that I was going to be a boy. So, my father picked out a boy's name. The problem was, SURPRISE, I came out a girl! What a disappointment for my father. So, I was given a boy's name that was even spelled the boy's way. My mother made sure I knew that my name was given to me to remind me that I was not wanted by my father. Later in life, when I was in my forties, I changed my name after God dealt with the pain of my father not wanting me. Needless to say, this disappointment resulted in my father ignoring me most of my younger years. Even though this was what life had handed me, I was a very happy child. I often stated that I lived in a "bubble" where life was pleasant and happy. I knew the abuse was going on, but I was always laughing, singing, and talking. This drove my dad crazy. He would often tell me that I was "insane" and needed to be committed. This ended up being a wound that God spent many years repairing inside of me.

I witnessed many forms of abuse: my brothers' fingers being burnt after playing with matches; my sister being punched in the eye and flung across the kitchen to hit the stove; my brother being given forty lashes with a belt after receiving forty demerits (bad marks) at school; my brothers being hit many times with a metal broom handle; my sister being kicked in the tail bone with pointy-toed cowboy boots; all the siblings being lined up on a couch and hit with a belt because one child did something wrong (I was never hit because by the time my father got to me I would be sobbing so hard that he would be exasperated and make the declaration, "forget it" and would leave me alone); and the list continues on. This behavior was just the physical abuse. I witnessed much verbal abuse from swearing to name calling. After becoming a Christian at twenty-six years old, I found out there was sexual abuse that went on in the family when we were young. My two younger sisters informed the family that one of my brothers sexually molested them (raped as was told to me) for approximately seven years. It started when they were seven and eight years old and did not end until the youngest was sixteen years old. My brother was approximately fourteen when it started and twenty one when it ended. My older sister informed me that my father used to wake up the girls early in the morning before work by touching their breasts. He did not come to my bed, but remember, he ignored me most of my life. I was shocked when I found out much of this information. I struggled to believe all of this information, so God revealed different things to me after I became a Christian. One came in the form of a letter from my aunt (after my uncle had passed away) informing me that my grandfather and his oldest daughter had sexually molested my father and his siblings. They were also severely beaten by my grandfather. He even beat his youngest son in the head with a board and caused him to have intellectual impairment. God also revealed to me that my mother was sexually molested by her brothers and her father used to call her horrible names because he did not want her. In addition, my great grandfather owned a prostitution brothel where he paid for the prostitutes' abortions. He was a very wealthy man, and he ultimately drove his wife insane and had her committed to an asylum where she birthed her final child. My grandmother ended up raising all her siblings and they were neglected and mistreated by their father. All of these revelations helped me to understand why my parents were the way they were. This did not make it any easier to accept but at least there were reasons. The one scenario that I ultimately had a hard time accepting was the one about my father touching my sisters' in the mornings. I prayed about this and the Lord used a strange circumstance to reveal to me that this was entirely possible. One day when I was at my parents' house my father was drunk. This was very strange because my father was not a drinker. My father asked me to give him a kiss. Now, this should have been a "red flag" to me because my father did not show me affection. I don't remember us children ever being told we were loved, and I did not receive any kisses or hugs from my father. Anyway, when he kissed me, it was a French kiss. I pulled away and told him to never touch me again. When I told my mother the incident, she sarcastically stated, "What! Do you want an apology from your father?" I immediately told her no but that he was not ever allowed to come near me again. When she confronted my father, he admitted to doing this. Later, I found out that when my sisters told my mother what my brother had been doing to them, she called them liars and never did anything to help those two young girls. It shouldn't have surprised me that she would do nothing to help me because she never helped them. Needless to say, I spent years having to forgive my parents for all these different kinds of abuse. I only relay all this information to set the stage of damage that can cause emotional and mental scars that could lead to depression.

Because of the control and abuse that I witnessed in my childhood home, I was desperate to "get out," so in September, 1981 I got married at the young age of 18 years old to John. Within the first sixteen months of my marriage I had my first child, Jean. Eleven months later my second child, John Jr., was born and ten months later my third, Lynn. Now, at the age of 21 years old I had three children under three and was very overwhelmed. Could this lead to suicide? Possibly, but not likely, so to understand what could, I would need to take you back to the first year of my marriage.

I was raised a Roman Catholic girl. Through the doctrine of the church, I was taught that goodness and good works got me to heaven. I was told that if I was a "good girl," God would take care of me, and my life would be good. I was afraid of God because I believed God to be a big, evil judge sitting in the sky waiting to condemn to hell anyone who committed a "mortal" sin because a mortal sin meant you were "bad." I worked extremely hard to be a "perfect" daughter and wife. I was a virgin when I met John, I did not touch any drugs, alcohol, or cigarettes, I did not swear, I did not lie, and I worked hard to help bring money into a spotless and perfect household. These were things that I was taught were qualities of a good wife and mother.

When John and I got married, he took me to another state to live by his parents. At that time, I thought he had quit drinking, smoking, and drugs. He lied to me, and I was so desperate to leave home that I believed him and was blinded to the truth. Within one week of moving out of state, I caught him doing drugs with his siblings, getting drunk every weekend, and gambling with his parents. He became possessive, jealous, and started to abuse me (physically and verbally). I caught him in bed with my best friend one night when I came home from work. When I confronted him, he told me that I deserved it because I was "sleeping around." I did not understand this because I was not doing such a terrible thing. I started saving my money so that I could move back to my home state. John lost his paychecks gambling and the only money to pay the bills was mine, so I would go without food for days because I wanted to save the little bit of money I had left out of my paychecks to return back to my home state. I ended up losing thirty pounds in nine months (which I couldn't afford), but I got to go back to my home state. Upon returning, things did not improve. I thought for sure that getting pregnant would force him to be mature, so we had children. This was a mistake because it only made things worse. The stress of providing for a family caused him to drink and use drugs even more, and he became even more possessive and controlling. He swore at me, called me terrible names (i.e. you @%#\>*^! # whore), forced sex upon me, emotionally and mentally abused me, threw things at me, and so forth. I even caught him "making out" in the field with one of my sisters. When confronted, he gave me the same explanation that I was previously given: I deserved this because I was having affairs – again, this was not true. The entire time all this was happening, I tried to go to church and follow God, but I became more depressed and angry with God because I thought He was not doing His part in my life. I became paranoid and would find myself doing crazy things like straightening my bed and couch right before John returned home from work. He would mark my tires to make sure I didn't go anywhere, so I would park the car in the exact same spot after I would go somewhere. I walked on egg shells to not make him angry. All this did not matter. Over seven years' time, he abused me in every way imaginable. Finally, the night he endangered my children's lives was the night I made him leave. He took my three children while I was at work. I had to get a job because we were going bankrupt because he gambled and drugged our money away. He got drunk and high and drove with my children and did not return with them until three o'clock in the morning. The kids informed me that he fell asleep while they played in the truck at a rest stop. They were two, three, and four years old. I was so angry, I kicked him out. I told him that to abuse me was one thing, but to endanger the lives of my children was something I could not tolerate. Shortly after making him leave, he came to my house and tried to kill me. My sister had moved in with me and she was being intimate with her boyfriend at my house. John and I used to use "emotion lotion" when we were intimate. My sister decided to use the bottle, but I did not know it. John had marked the bottle so he could prove I was having affairs on him. When he stopped at my house to see the kids that day, he found that some of the lotion had been used. He sent the kids to the neighbor's house, and when I came home he threw me on a bed and started to choke me to death. I do not know how I got away, but it must have been adrenaline because I threw him off of me and ran to the phone to call 911. He ran out because I threatened to have him arrested. The next day my throat had bruises and was swollen. I had the locks changed, but he returned to my house the next day only to threaten to kill me when he got in. I called the police and had to be escorted out of the city to my parents' house. This kind of behavior continued for eight months, and I got more depressed and lonely. I tried to date John the first four months he was gone; we even went to marriage counseling. In addition, I went to the family portion of drug counseling (while he was at his drug counseling) to try and understand his behavior. Everything failed, and his counselor told me that John loved drugs and had no intention of quitting. I got very angry because I had come to the end of all solutions that I could think of. I told God that I did not believe in Him anymore because He had let my life fall apart. I felt He failed me because as I saw it, He had promised to take care of me and my life was in great crisis. What I did not understand was that God did not promise to "save" me because of my good works; Catholic doctrine taught me this. The truth is, salvation comes as a free gift from God and has nothing to do with our good works. "For it is by grace you have been saved, through faith- and this is not from yourselves, it is the gift of God- not by works, so that no one can boast" (Ephesians 2:8-9). God takes care of one because He loves His creation. Because I did not understand this concept, I got angry with God and turned away from Him. During the time that I left God, I started to sin heavily and the next four months became the darkest, loneliest and most desperate times of my life. I was so lonely, and I lacked the love I needed. I turned to lots of men to find my peace, joy and love. Why wouldn't I? I was sure that is what my ex-husband thought of me anyway (at least that is what he always told me). Needless to say, I didn't find love, joy or peace. Instead, I found pain and misery. I prostituted my body for this period of time for the measly cost of a meal so that I could eat. The greatest cost came to my soul. I became more desperate and lonely. My soul got darker and there was a vast emptiness and void where I should have been putting Jesus Christ, not men. I was exhausted mentally and emotionally; trying to raise kids during the day and work at night was destroying my physical body as well. One cannot possibly live on three to four hours of sleep each night for a year. I didn't eat because I was sick from being so tired. Soon, I began to lose a lot of weight and ended up at a doctor who told me to change my life, or I would die. I tried this with counseling but was not successful because I couldn't possibly find what I needed from a human being.

As the sin got greater, my very existence seemed to be worth nothing to me. The loneliness consumed me; the more men I had the lonelier I got. I could not see any way out. I remember being in a dark, endless pit; a whirlwind of sin, to say the least. This whirlwind sucked me into a hole that I could not seem to get out of. I once heard a pastor say that "sin would take you farther than you wanted to go, keep you longer than you wanted to stay, and cost you more than you wanted to pay." This quote was coming true in my life. It had been four months of incredible sin and darkness, and I was sick and tired of my sin. The devil was using my own loneliness, hopelessness, and rebellion to God to destroy my life. Scripture tells us "Stay alert! Watch out for your great enemy, the devil. He prowls around like a roaring lion, looking for someone to devour" (1 Peter 5:8). The devil was sure accomplishing all he had set out to do – devour my children and me. During this time my children were living in more stress than any children could possibly be expected to endure. My son was misbehaving terribly, my oldest daughter cried every time I left her, and my youngest daughter was awful and sassy in order to receive some sort of attention.

The life I was living was a disgrace to me and my children, so I kept it a secret. I started living a double life; during the week I was a good mom, but when the kids went with their father I would become the harlot. I even kept two wardrobes in order to live my split life. I never did the drugs or alcohol because, not only was I afraid of them, but I had lived with them too long and they had caused too much damage in my life. So, men became my outlet, married or single it did not matter, they were simply a way out! This brought me to desperation and to the point of explaining why I was sitting on a bed contemplating suicide. I wanted the least painful way to do this, but I was scared, so I cried out to God for help. I stated to Him, "If you are there, and I mean IF, please send me some help." This help came in the form of the thought I previously shared with you: "If I killed myself, my three children would have to live with a drug addict." I couldn't bear that thought. After I became a Christian, I understood that God put that thought in my head so that I wouldn't go through with suicide. Anyway, I woke up the next morning and by the grace of God I didn't kill myself, but I was still the same desperate, lonely person. I trudged through the next few weeks.

After those few weeks, God sent the answer to my cry – my husband, Louis, came into my life. I was a cocktail waitress across the street from the restaurant where he worked, and he was waiting tables this particular night. I always went over to this restaurant to have toast and cocoa after my shift was over. I worked the bar rush, so it was about two o'clock in the morning when I got off work. I had a guy friend that knew Louis. I remember when my friend asked me if I would like to meet a guy; I told him no because I had vowed men off after all the pain of the last few months. I was sure that all men wanted from me was sex. I was at the table with one of my co-workers that had joined me and my guy friend when Louis came over to take our order. He didn't say much, he introduced himself and then took our order. After he left I said to my co-worker, "did you feel that thing?" She said, "What thing?" Then she told me she thought I just wanted to have sex with him. I told her that I didn't. I looked at her and stated, "You mean you didn't feel that thing?" She again stated that she didn't know what I was talking about. When Louis came back to our table I felt it again and had no idea what it was. After giving my life to Jesus Christ I realized that what I felt, at that time, was the love of Jesus tugging at me. I remember when I felt this strange feeling, I was thinking that this man was so gentle and kind and had so much peace that I just wanted to be with him. Anyway, after my co-worker left, my guy friend completely ignored what I had said and introduced me to Louis. We ended up talking until about six o'clock in the morning. While we were chatting, Louis asked me on a date several times and each time I told him no, even though I noticed a remarkable difference in him from other men. Finally, he walked me out to my car and one last time asked me on a date. I turned him down again, so he finally turned to walk away. When he did this, I rolled down my window and told him I would go out with him. He was so baffled that he asked me what had changed my mind. I told him it was because he had not tried to kiss me. Louis looked at me with disbelief and chuckled and said, "Why would I do that, I don't even know you?" I simply stated, "That had not stopped any man before." This started our dating relationship. We had decided to not include sex into this relationship because Louis would feel too much guilt. For the next year and three months we dated. Louis spent every day or evening with me and eventually my children so he could get to know us.

From August until December, Louis preached to me every day. We rarely talked about anything but Jesus. I once said to him, "Don't you know anything else to talk about but Jesus?" He simply replied, "No! Not until you get saved." I did not understand what this meant, but whatever this meant; I knew it meant we would continue to discuss the Bible and Jesus. As we continued to discuss Jesus in depth, God started doing his miraculous work. One night we were lying on the bed discussing the book of Revelation and I asked Louis if I was going to go to heaven. He very bluntly stated,

"No, you're going straight to hell!" That scared me because I didn't want to go to hell; I wanted to be one of those people we had talked about that went up to meet Jesus in the air (referred to as the Rapture). While we were lying there, Louis had his hand on the back of my neck and inside of his head he told me he was silently praying the name of Jesus. While he did this, a demon left me. Scripture states in Mark 16:17-18, "And these signs will accompany those who believe: in my name they will cast out demons . . . ." Louis believed, so when he prayed, "In Jesus' Name," the demon left me. I was about fifteen years old when this demon entered into me. It was a beautiful red-head woman that I used to talk with. Whenever I had intercourse with a man, she would be there to talk with me and in my mind I would have intercourse with her. Years later when the Lord had me start helping others get free of demons, He explained to me that the "she" demon had entered into me through the years of reading and watching pornography. I started doing this when I was fifteen when I read filthy sex stories in magazines my mother owned. By the time I was eighteen and married, John had me watching pornographic films every Friday and Saturday night and then would have me act out what we watched. To get back to the demon leaving me – what happened was so amazing. A huge hand appeared in my head and shut this "she-demon" behind a door. I began to call out to her in my mind and asked her where she went and she said, "He has shut me behind the door and I can't come out." I asked this demon who had shut her behind the door. Her reply was "Jesus Christ." I sat up in bed and at that instant, in the mirror by my bed; Jesus appeared! I remember yelling at Louis in anger saying, "What did you do to me?" I didn't understand what had just happened. All I knew was that someone who had lived in me for a very long time was just taken from me and that felt like a big hole in my soul. I believed that this "demon" was my friend and was there to help me. Louis simply stated to me that I was just delivered from a demon. Then, of all things, he got up and left the house which left me alone with God. I was very confused but I knew one thing: I needed to be "saved" as Louis had put it. I needed Jesus to come and fix my life and fill the void that was left from all the men, me turning from God and telling Him I didn't need Him, and from the deliverance that had just happened. I did what any confused person would do (ha, ha), I opened the Bible to the book of Revelation and read it three times through until I believe I understood it. I knew Louis was right and that I would go to hell. After reading the book, I knelt by my bed and said a very "pathetic" attempt at a salvation prayer. Good thing God doesn't care about reciting fancy prayers – He just needs a person who is sincere and talks to Him. I told Jesus I had screwed up my life and I needed Him to come and take over. At that instant there was a change inside of me and I felt such peace. That was something I had not had in about eight years. There was a sweet love that took over me. I immediately changed – I stopped swearing, having sex, and doing anything else that I thought would displease the Lord. 2 Corinthians 5:17 states, "Therefore, if anyone is in Christ, the new creation has come: The old has gone, the new is here!" I was definitely a new creation at that moment. I let Christ come in and take over my heart and my life. After I prayed and the change happened, I saw a vision of myself in the very outer courts of the throne room of God. I desperately wanted to be at the throne, but couldn't get there because of all these people around the throne. Then a huge hand of light (the same one that shut the demon behind the door) reached over the crowd and picked me up and put me at the foot of the throne of God. I then heard a voice say, "Lily, you will stay here at the foot of the throne for eternity." I knew then that God had heard my prayer, and He had saved me. I knew that whatever God asked of me, I would do. I had vowed my life and faithfulness to Him. At that very moment, I knew that my God had vowed His faithfulness to me and would never leave nor forsake me no matter what happened. God has, in every way possible, been there for me. This night began an incredible journey of Louis and me walking through multiple trials, tribulations, pain and grief. As I share the tribulations, know that I am sharing not only to relay the faithfulness of God through trials that demand complete reliance on Him, but to show you, the reader, that God can do the same in your life as you walk through pain, grief, sorrow, anger, and many other feelings and heartaches that may seem unbearable. The coming chapters will bring stories of multiple raging storms ranging from divorce, death of a first-born child and grandson, a son going off to Iraq war, a daughter in drugs and sexual immortality who eventually took my grandchildren from me and entered witchcraft, terminal illness, death of my ex-husband and death of my second husband, spiritual abuse by various churches and pastors, and finally the sexual molestation and impregnation of my minor daughter by a Christian counselor. These may seem like unbearable trials brought on back to back, but these chapters will also bring stories of incredible miracles, signs, and wonders (visits to heaven), redemption, salvation, comfort, healing, forgiveness, hope, and love. As you read through these chapters, I pray that you will learn that weeping, sorrow, pain, and tears are all instruments that God can use to refine and bless while glorifying Jesus. Isaiah 61:3 is an incredible passage to stand upon, ". . . and (He) will provide for those who grieve in Zion – to bestow on them a crown of beauty instead of ashes, the oil of joy instead of mourning, and a garment of praise instead of a spirit of despair. They will be called oaks of righteousness, a planting of the Lord for the display of his splendor." This is a scripture that Louis and I stood on many times knowing that God would take all of our pain, mourning, despair, and any other sorrow we endured and turn it into splendor for Him.

# CHAPTER II

# CYCLONE DIVORCE & DEATH

When one is ready to be completely healed, God starts the process. He is faithful to finish what He starts, so the first job at hand was to save and heal my family. My three little ones needed to be healed of the effects of divorce and needed to hear the Word of God so that they could accept Christ as their savior. Shortly after my salvation, Jean, my oldest daughter, got saved. It happened on a night when I was at work and Louis was watching them. He had played the song "Jesus Loves Me" by the Bill Gaither Trio. When the song was playing, Louis and the three kids were worshipping and praying and Jean asked Jesus to be her Savior. The following morning she ran downstairs and jumped on my bed excitedly and started to relay the story of the night before. She told me about how when she asked Jesus into her heart, she saw Him open up her heart and take her hand and walk her through her heart into heaven. She said, "We were walking in a garden!" She continued to tell me all about the butterflies and flowers that were in heaven. Then she told me that Jesus promised her she would live with Him forever in heaven. She told me that all the pain in her heart from her daddy leaving was now gone. Jesus was faithful to heal her from the divorce. Shortly after that John Jr. and Lynn accepted Jesus, and He healed their hearts from the divorce also. We were far from finished, there was a lot of pain that needed to be healed, but Jesus had started the process, and I knew that He would finish it. The Word of God confirmed my beliefs in Philippians 1:6, "For I am confident of this very thing, that He who began a good work in you will perfect it until the day of Christ Jesus."

From the day of my salvation, January 7, 1990, until the day I married Louis, approximately a year later, God had much work to do. Besides salvation, there was spiritual cleaning that had to be completed so the Lord could put the gifts and fruits of the Spirit inside me. I would need these gifts in order to survive the trials that were ahead. The first deliverance was from anger. There was so much anger from my childhood and the abuse from my first husband that I found myself mad, even furious, at even small things. The deliverance came at a home church meeting Louis and I were attending. I shared about all the anger I was experiencing and so the leader's wife offered prayer. She and the others started praying and I could feel the anger leave me. I felt as if sharp objects were being thrown out of me. Once the prayer was over, I felt a peace take over my whole body. That was something that I don't ever remember experiencing. The leader's wife told me that she had seen a vision of a bunch of sharp articles like knives, scissors, and so forth being thrown out of me and then she saw peace flow in. I shared that it was exactly what I felt had happened to me. I explained that as fast as the sharp objects left, I felt love, gentleness, and peace flow into me. To this day God is still working on anger in different situations. It is a struggle that I continue to try and conquer. As I had to forgive different church leaders from spiritual abuse throughout the last fifteen years, I have struggled to not allow anger to rule my emotions. Anger is not my primary emotion anymore; I feel other emotions such as sadness, frustration, disappointment, and so forth. Before God did any work, anger was all I ever experienced. I don't believe I could feel other emotions because anger was always present. I am always quick to repent if I sin while angry. Anger is not the sin; it is how one reacts in the anger that is sin. When one experiences the need to hurt, cause pain, seek revenge, grudge hold, and then bitterness results, then one is sinning. God knew one would get angry and so that is why He commanded, "In your anger do not sin": Do not let the sun go down while you are still angry" (Ephesians 4:26). Be quick to repent, ask forgiveness, and resolve with the one you are angry with. This is a very good way to keep bitterness from taking root in your heart.

The next deliverance was a lustful demon. Many things came as a result of the pornography in my first marriage, at the time of my salvation, the homosexual demon had left, but the desire to masturbate had not. This had become a terrible addiction in my life. No matter how fulfilled I was in my sexual life, I still had the urge to masturbate. Time and again I tried to take care of this problem myself but could not. I finally came to the point where I truly hated this sin. When that happened I begged the Lord to take this sin away. I repented for the pornography in my first marriage, and God was faithful to forgive me and the desire to masturbate immediately stopped. When one is involved with pornography various demonic spirits and sins come with the territory. If left in this long enough, it will destroy or will bring unnatural desires, such as homosexuality.

If you are faithful to repent, there is no sin too big for the Lord to forgive and bring full deliverance.

While all this deliverance was happening, I was watching the Lord work out the details of my upcoming marriage to Louis. I was watching Louis walk his Christian walk and was learning how to love and give to others. One of the first acts of love that I witnessed from Louis was when he gave me all the money he had saved so that I could pay off debt left by my previous husband. Even before he asked me to marry him, he had only known me a few weeks, he handed me all his savings. He had saved about $25,000 in order to return to college for his Masters in Theology. He knew that I was losing my house and drowning in debt from my first husband's stupid financial decisions. He went to the bank, withdrew all the money, and told me to pay off all my debt and hire a lawyer so that I could be free from John's abuse. Needless to say, I was crying and speechless. I could not begin to pay this man back $25,000. When I told him this he stated that even if I never seen him again, I would never have to return the money. I had witnessed one of the greatest acts of love that I had ever seen. This man handed over his life's savings to a poor, destitute, single mom in order to save her house from being repossessed and her heat and telephone from being shut off. I accepted the money but could not understand the concept of this love. I took part of the money and hired an attorney. Eventually I agreed to marry Louis, but I had a desperate struggle going on inside of me. I knew the Lord hated divorce. I realized God's ultimate goal was salvation and restoration. I believed God ultimately wanted to save marriages and not end them. I prayed and asked the Lord if He wanted me to marry Louis, and I believe He spoke into my heart and told me to. His exact words to me were, "Not only do you love Louis, but you will go wherever I send him." As Louis asked me to marry him several times, I did not say yes right away because I was not sure if I loved him. I did not understand love because I had never experienced real love in my first marriage, so how could I begin to understand "real committed love?" My struggle with getting divorced continued. As I read scripture, I realized that the Bible said if I married Louis I would cause him to commit adultery because he was marrying a divorced woman. Finally, the Lord used a teaching by Derek Prince called, "Divorce, Remarriage, and Celibacy" in order to deliver me from guilt, heal my heart from divorce, and free me to marry Louis.

While listening to this tape, the presence of God filled the room. I felt God say to me, "It is time to be healed and delivered." Repentance, sobbing, cleansing, and finally release came. God's faithfulness to heal my guilt and pain was again shown through His Word and the mercy and grace of God. I knew then that God wanted me to marry Louis in order to bless my life and restore damage done from a seven year bad marriage. He was binding me to a believer. It was time to give Louis the "yes" answer he had been waiting for. The way in which I was able to give him the "yes" answer was, in my eyes, God's way of using simple circumstances in life to confirm what He wanted as well as use His sense of humor to show us that He can be a "fun" God as well. Louis and I went to a Chinese restaurant to eat. While we were there, I broke open my fortune cookie (just to clarify that God does not want us to seek our fortune through fortune-telling avenues) only to find it to say "accept the next proposal you hear." I was astounded at such a strange coincidence, so I put the piece of paper in my purse. When I excused myself to go to the bathroom, Louis found my fortune and when I returned he held up the paper and asked me to marry him. He said, "you can't say no because your fortune said you must accept the next proposal you hear." I laughed so hard and then told him that I would marry him not because of some fortune cookie because I did not believe in those, but because God had instructed me to say yes a few nights earlier. The entire place cheered when they watched this happen. I would reiterate that I think God has a funny sense of humor. Of course, He would use something like a fortune cookie to confirm what He wanted to happen.

As time progressed there were many other damaged areas of my life that needed healing: physically, emotionally, spiritually, and mentally. One area of physical healing that needed to be accomplished was in the area of my vocal chords. My ex-husband and I used to verbally fight and have screaming battles. During one of these screaming fights I lost my voice for six weeks. There was absolutely no noise coming out. I went to an ENT doctor, and he told me I had damaged my vocal chords very badly. He said all the screaming had given me nodules and my vocal chords were bruised and swollen to such an extent they would not vibrate any more. He prescribed me medication and sent me home. They got a little better over time but then if I overworked my voice at all they would shut off again. I struggled with bouts of Laryngitis for about six years. I finally ended up at the ENT doctor again and he came up with the same diagnosis and told me that surgery would need to be done. Surgery meant a knife would cut off the nodules. The doctor informed me that if he happened to slip and make a mistake I would never speak again. That was horrifying to me! I LOVE to talk and sing and that thought terrified me. When I got home I told Louis we needed to pray. This was on a Friday and the surgery was scheduled for Monday. I was anointed with oil at church and there was prayer for my vocal chords and miraculously God healed them. The Word of God states, "Is anyone among you sick? Let them call the elders of the church to pray over them and anoint them with oil in the name of the Lord (James 5:14). When one is obedient to the Word and has faith, God can heal that individual miraculously. I still had a surgery scheduled, so on Monday I returned to the same ENT doctor and told him that I wanted him to check my vocal chords again before proceeding with the surgery. He took the scope and went down my throat and declared that all the nodules were gone, the swelling and bruising was gone, and my vocal chords were normal. He was astounded and asked me what had happened. I told him that I had prayer, and he declared that I was healed and had received a miracle.

The surgery was canceled, and he told me to go home. Sometimes when God does a healing, He leaves some sort of a sign to remind us not to sin again. I was left with the struggle of Laryngitis whenever I raised my voice or yelled, and I could no longer sing. I was frustrated with this whole thing because I loved to sing. After struggling for a few years, I begged God to take this problem from me. I wanted to be able to sing worship songs. So on a Sunday night at church, I went up for prayer for the complete restoration of my vocal chords. One of the women at the church came up to pray for me. She told me God gave her a word, but that it was a hard word. She told me He had instructed her to tell me to not speak for three days, and He would heal my vocal chords. That was a daunting task for me because I had six children and twins on the way (three of them under two at the time). I needed my voice more than ever. I told her that I was willing but that I did not know how I could possibly adhere to this command. We prayed for God's help and what happened was amazing. I fell under the power of God, and He completely shut off my vocal chords. Not one sound came out for three whole days. I spoke through writing notes and clapping hands at my children. At the end of three days it was Wednesday evening and we were going to a church worship celebration; I was confused because God had promised me my voice back completely healed at the end of the three days. I shared my disappointment with my husband, and he encouraged me to continue to believe. When everyone was in the car, I had forgotten my purse in the house, so through a written note I told Louis that I needed to go in the house and get it. When I entered the door I was forced down to my knees under the power of God; I heard the Lord say, "SPEAK FORTH, WOMAN." When I opened my mouth my voice was completely back. It was strong and clear. I tried out singing but still there was no noise. The Lord spoke to my heart and told me to continue to have faith. When we got to the worship celebration the first song came on and the Lord spoke to me and told me to open my mouth and sing. As soon as I did, there was beautiful singing (at least I thought it was) coming out of my mouth. Once again, damage from a terrible marriage was restored and healed. It took about six years and many lessons, but the Lord completed the healing. Again, He was faithful to complete a good work He had started in me. Again, Philippians 1:6 states that we can be confident of this, "that he who began a good work in you will carry it on to completion until the day of Christ Jesus."

As God was working on healing the various areas in my children and my life, He was also working on getting Louis and I married. One of the most amazing miracles God did was in December of 1990. Shortly before this the Lord had told me the exact date He wanted us to get married; in faith, I set the date. I told my lawyer this and she said she would do her best but the courts were backed up through August, 1991. I told her to try her best and if God wanted it to happen he would work it out. December came and so did the phone call. My lawyer called and told me that, as she thought, the soonest we could get in was August. I knew the Lord had told me the exact date, which was in January 1991 and it was not August 1991. I stood firm and told her to try once again, and I prayed. About the third week of December she called me back and told me that I wasn't going to believe what had happened. She stated that she got a court date for December 28th. I was so stunned that I asked her how she did it. She told me that she had told the clerk of court I had financial difficulties (which was true), and I needed to be divorced before the end of the year. Without hesitation the clerk agreed to put me in and "lo and behold" I was granted a divorce on December 28th. The Lord added blessings because my ex-husband did not show up for the court date, and I was granted everything I asked for. I got the house, the kids, and child support was granted. On December 31st the divorce was filed. I did not know at the time, but there was a five-day wait for a marriage certificate. On January 2nd, because of New Years' they weren't open on January 1st, I went to get my divorce certificate and my marriage license. It was kind of comical because when I showed up at the desk to pick up my divorce papers, I asked the clerk where I went for a marriage license and she pointed to the other side of the counter and told me right there. I walked two feet over to the right and asked for a marriage license. She had the most stunned look on her face. I explained that it was not what she was thinking. She asked me the date we were getting married and when I told her that it was only three days away, she told me that it was impossible. When I asked why, she told me that there was a five day wait. The earliest I could get married was in five days. I explained to her that God had spoken to me and told me that we were to get married in three days, so I needed to know how to bypass the wait. She told me that there was no way to do that, but then in the next breath told me that she would give me a list of the judges and we could pick one and ask if the wait period could be waived. She stated that they would never do this, but I could try. I took the list home and Louis and I prayed over it and picked the judge we believed the Lord wanted. We were going to ask the same judge to marry us but this was not what God had in mind.

The Sunday before any of this took place, December 30th, I was in church and the Lord told me to ask the pastor to marry us. I couldn't believe this because we were getting married in six days. The Lord spoke to me and told me that this was Louis' first marriage and he deserved a pastor to marry him. After service, I obediently asked the pastor to marry us. He agreed and asked me when we wanted to be married. When I said "This Saturday" he was so surprised. He stated that there was normally a six month class to attend but that he would need to talk with us and could possibly waive it. This brought on a meeting between the pastor, Louis, and me. God worked miraculously on that Wednesday evening. The pastor asked many questions about why we were getting married. When it came time to question me, he asked why my parents were not attending the ceremony. I explained that when I became a Christian and stopped going to the Catholic Church, they disowned me. My mother actually told me that I had to choose between, what she called, "My Jesus" or being their daughter. In one second I chose Jesus. They did not speak to me for approximately 20 years after that. They also made it clear that if I married Louis they would not come to the wedding. They were convinced that he was pulling me away from the Catholic Church. After a few hours of questioning us, the pastor waived the six month wait period. That was one of the mountains God moved to let us get married on that Saturday. The next came in the form of a meeting with the judge.

Louis and I called the judge we believed God had revealed on the list and asked if he would meet with us; he agreed. Louis met with the judge on Tuesday. The judge asked Louis why he wanted to marry me. Louis relayed the story of how he had been a bachelor up until now and he was thirty-five years old. He shared how God had told him I would be his wife, which happened in the restaurant the night we met. God pointed me out to Louis and told him that I would be his wife and how God orchestrated our meeting. He told the judge how much he loved me and had "saved" himself for me.

Louis was a virgin because he had waited for his wife all these years. The judge concluded that Louis obviously loved me very much and that he would make his decision once he talked to me. On Wednesday morning I met with the judge. He explained that Louis had told him how much he loved me and asked me if I loved him just as much. I told him yes, and he told me that we were obviously old enough to know what we wanted. In addition, he told me that he was so impressed with Louis' story and how he had waited 35 years for a wife and kept pure that he would waive the five-day wait so we could get married on the appointed day. Again, God had intervened for us to be married on the day He ordained. God's hand seemed to be on everything about this wedding, including the planning. Because Louis and I had planned on a judge, we had nothing planned for this wedding and it was two days away. The pastor helped us, and we ended up with a guitarist (the assistant pastor) and a pianist (his daughter). I did not have a dress, and when I told my neighbor I was getting married, she borrowed me a brand new dress from Macy's (tags still on). Louis' two good friends stood up as the Best Man and Matron of Honor. The wedding consisted of Louis, my three children, his two friends, the pastor, and me. After the wedding, it was time to sign the license; one of the children asked, "Don't we get to sign that, we were married too you know." The pastor turned over the license and let them sign the back. This was correct. That day we were all married and became one family. On top of all of this, the pastor presented us with a night at the Holiday Inn honeymoon suite and his wife made us a beautiful table cloth.

The Lord had supplied all of our needs and brought us to this wonderful point in our life. The Word of God states, "Now to him who is able to do immeasurably more than all we ask or imagine, according to his power that is at work within us" (Ephesians 3:20). God had not only supplied our needs but had gone above and beyond what I could have asked for in this wedding planning. Now that we were married, there was refining work to be accomplished. There were years of bitterness and forgiveness toward my ex-husband that needed to be taken care of. All the years of abuse and torment had left me with hatred in my heart and a wish that God would kill John, so I would not have to deal with him anymore. I used to ask that a truck would run him over or something of the like. When someone has abused you long enough, this type of thinking seems the logical solution to stop the pain. This type of desire is called malice (to cause extreme harm to someone); the Lord commands us to remove this from our heart. "Let all bitterness and wrath and anger and clamor and slander be put away from you, along with all malice. Be kind to one another, tenderhearted, forgiving one another, as God in Christ forgave you" (Ephesians 4:31-12). I could not accomplish this on my own, so God, in His kindness, started to help me through this process. Forgiveness is a decision, but it can also be a continual process. I had stated many times that I forgave John, but I could not feel this in my heart. The decision had been made, but God needed to work out the feeling. This came one particular weekend when John had taken the three children on a Friday evening. He was supposed to return them on Saturday evening but did not show up. He called and stated that he was not going to return the kids. When I asked him what he meant, he stated he had no intention of ever returning the kids. Now, when you tell a woman you aren't returning her children, she becomes slightly hysterical. I started yelling at him and told him he had better bring them back now. He hung up on me. I drove the hour and a half to where he lived, and when I got there he had the children locked in his house and wouldn't even let them see me. They were at the window crying, still he refused to let them come out or me go in. I ended up having to leave without my kids; when I returned home it was very late. I called the police and explained the situation to them. The next morning the police officer called John and explained that if he did not return the children by evening there would be kidnapping charges filed against him. I still did not know if he intended to bring the children back, so I went to church with Louis. I thought for sure I had forgiven my ex-husband at least a thousand times for everything he had done to me. There were months of stalking my home for hours and hours, calling my work and accusing me of terrible things to my boss, times where he stood in my yard yelling and swearing at me so the neighbors could hear, breaking down the door of a friend to get to me, taking me to court that cost thousands of dollars only to hear him lie to the judge, lying to my children about me, and the list goes on and on. The new problem: here I was again with anger, hurt, bitterness, and unforgiveness filling up my very being. What do you think the sermon was on that morning? "FORGIVENESS!" Of all subjects for the pastor to speak on – Forgiveness. The pastor spoke about how the Word of God states that we are to forgive someone seven times seventy (Matthew 18:22). The pastor reiterated that we are to do this daily. The pastor asked the question, "Can anyone offend you 490 times a day?" I turned to Louis and said to him, "He has never lived with my ex!" All of the sudden, I found myself crying and the Lord was speaking to me and telling me I had to forgive John again. There were about 300 people in that church that day. We were sitting in the center of a row in the back. There was no way that the pastor could have seen me through the crowd. Right after he finished the sermon, the pastor sought me out. He had no idea what had happened since Friday evening. Before I could say anything, he looked at me and told me that the Lord wanted to heal my heart from unforgiveness, and if I would receive it, He would do it. I began to sob. I was so broken that I gladly let God take over and do what He needed to do in order to "fix" my heart. One more time I forgave my ex-husband. The true test of the work God did that day was not far on the horizon. The Lord did a work in my heart that Sunday which allowed me to be able to trust Him in difficult situations and respond in faith and not anger. The test came later in the form of a packet in the mail from an attorney filled with lies and accusations. Another court date had been set, and Louis and I were out of money. We had tapped all our resources dry through the various court battles trying to save our children.

When the packet arrived, it was filled with exaggerated truths and gregarious lies. I became extremely angry and started to cry. My three children were pre-teens at this time, so they read the affidavit. They realized their father had told many lies inside of this paper, but this did not make it any easier to forgive him. Once again, I found myself on my face in repentance for hating my ex-husband. I found myself again wishing him dead because I felt I had lived enough torment from this man. I figured I had reaped enough consequences for the sins I had sowed. Once I had settled down, God gently spoke to my heart and told me I needed to forgive him once again for all he had done to me. This seemed like it should be a simple thing, but in the packet there were not only lies but my ex-husband asked for the maximum penalty for contempt of court; that would be time in jail. Louis helped me through this time of turmoil and rationally told me that we needed to ask God to intervene. The next morning I searched for an attorney; I called a counseling place and asked for a list of lawyers. When I got the list, Louis and I prayed over it and we felt as if a name jumped out at us. We called the attorney who ended up being a Christian family law attorney of twenty-some years. After hearing the case he told me it was "in the bag." He drew up papers which ended up costing around five thousand dollars. As I stated before, Louis and I had tapped all our resources dry, so we ended up using money that my family had given to us for the children's college education.

When the day of court finally arrived, Louis and I had prayed for intervention from God. I had run out of money for the lawyer, so I was physically in court by myself (even though God was present with me). I sat with papers in hand ready to defend myself without a lawyer. Before I explain what God did to intervene, I need to take you back in time to when I hired an attorney for my divorce. The day the divorce was final the attorney told me that she thought my ex-husband was a snake in the grass and suggested I kept a journal of all he said and did over the years when he took my kids. I heeded her advice, and God was able to use this journal to intervene in court the day I sat by myself.  My ex-husband, not knowing this existed, wasn't able to tell his lawyer about it, so the journal verified to the lawyer that many of his statements written in the paper were lies. I had written proof of his entire visitation with the kids week by week.

So, while sitting in front of the judge, before anything happened, his lawyer stood up and announced they were dropping all the charges against me. I was so shocked I could hardly speak. God had just freed me from possible jail in a matter of seconds. God used a previous lawyer's advice to set me free. So, if you find yourself in a predicament where you think there is no way out – trust the Lord. He can help. The Word of God states, "When you are brought before synagogues, rulers and authorities do not worry about how you will defend yourselves or what you will say. For the Holy Spirit will teach you in that very hour what you ought to say" (Luke 12:11). When you trust in the Lord, He will, not only, defend you but He will teach you what to do and what to say. After the court hearing though, John and I were ordered to go to intervention. While I was in intervention, I found myself in the same awful place of anger, bitterness, and unforgiveness. When I went to church that week, I found myself at an "altar call" where I was crying hysterically and screaming, "OKAY GOD, I FORGIVE HIM. EVERYTHING HE HAS EVER DONE, I FORGIVE HIM." At that moment the Lord cleansed me from my sins and freed me from those awful feelings that I had stored up for years. The Word of God tells us how to pray; we all know it as the *Our Father*. During this pray we ask God to "forgive us our trespasses as we forgive those who trespass against us." As one says this prayer, the thought of "who am I not to forgive someone when the Lord has forgiven me for so much?" should be rolling through one's head. If you are hanging onto bitterness and unforgiveness I believe the Lord would say: "Let it go – forgive as I have forgiven you." If you do this, there will be total restoration of your heart and mind. I know that when I finally forgave John, I found complete healing of my emotions from all the years of pain. I explained earlier that forgiveness is a decision, but it is also a process that needs to be completed. Philippians 1:6 states, ". . . being confident of this, that he who began a good work in you will carry it on to completion until the day of Christ Jesus." I am by no means saying that you will never feel anger, bitterness, irritation, or frustration in difficult situations again, but what I am saying is that those horrible thoughts and feelings will not rule your heart and mind anymore and forgiveness will come easier and easier.

    Louis used to tell me that John was just a man who needed salvation and that I needed to pray for him. This was such an amazing statement coming from him because when Louis met me and married me, he took over raising John's three kids (physically, emotionally, mentally, and spiritually) and paid off $30,000 of John's debt. Louis never complained nor said an unkind word about John. Whenever God threw a trial our way concerning John, he would just remind me that God had our best in mind and that He would be with us; all we needed to do was seek God and pray. Louis, John's three children, and I prayed for John numerous times over the years and asked God to save him. We got to see these prayers answered some 20 years later.

When God ripped out this bitterness and unforgiveness, He also replaced it with love for John's soul. This was something I never thought could happen in my life again. I found that I did not want to see him harmed or dead anymore. As I stated, my family prayed for John for many years. John died in 2011 from a horrible cancer. The testimony that comes with this death is not only incredible, but it testifies of the faithfulness and glory of God in the lives of even those who are unbelievers. The story was told to me this way: March 2011, John (55 years old) was at the casino when suddenly he started bumping into walls. John was a regular at the casino because gambling was one of his many addictions. (A pertinent piece of information that helps one to understand this story: John smoked about 15 joints of marijuana daily from about 13 years old on, drank quite a bit of alcohol, and smoked 2 packs of cigarettes per day). When he was asked his name, address, and if he had a family he did not know the answers to these questions. He was taken to the U of M hospital in an ambulance. He was given a brain and then body scan; they found that he had about 20 brain tumors, 20 lung tumors and cancer in all his major organs. Upon discovery, they informed John Jr. and Lynn that he had approximately 6 months to live. Within a day his condition worsened and they told the children he had approximately 6 weeks to live. The next day they told the children he had approximately 6 days to live. The doctors told John Jr. and Lynn that it was the fastest growing cancer they had ever seen in that hospital. When John realized he would be dying very soon, he asked John Jr. if he could speak with me. I need to let you know that John had never remarried because he told his children that he had never loved another woman besides me. I had only seen John twice in twelve years: once at Jean's funeral (our oldest daughter) and about a year before he was diagnosed with this cancer. I will later tell the incredible story of our daughter's death and funeral.

The second time was about a year before this diagnosis during which we spoke of Jean's death and my salvation. I was able to minister to him about Jean's death only being an accident and how he needed to forgive himself and how the change in me came from giving my life to Jesus Christ. He was now lying in a hospital bed facing death and the decision to give his life to Jesus Christ.

I went to the hospital with Louis, and we ended up preaching the gospel to John and praying the salvation prayer with him. I found it incredible that the very man who had preached to John's children and ex-wife and watched their salvation was now preaching to him and watching his salvation. For the next six days we helped John Jr. and Lynn walk through the death of their father. We read the Bible to John each day and night and prayed over him continually. Because his salvation was an end of life salvation, I questioned God on whether this was a valid salvation or was it just a desperate plea in the fear of death. I asked God to give us all a sign that this was true salvation and that John was going to be in heaven when he passed on to the next life. The answer came to me in this dream:
*I was sitting on the hospital bed with John. He kept telling me had to show me something in the family room. I kept telling him that*

*could not leave the room because I had to pray. He asked Louis and his two children, John Jr. and Lynn, to go into the family room with him. When he got out of the bed and started taking them to the family room to show them, he stressed that I needed to understand what was in the family room. When they walked in the family room there was a mantle that was wine colored on the bottom and gold on the top.* I woke up and asked God for the interpretation of the dream. He told me that the family room represented John's family. Louis and John's kids were in the family room and the mantle was representative of the covering of God. The wine color represented the blood of Jesus and the gold represented heaven. God told me that John had to pass through the mantle of the blood of Jesus in order to enter heaven. I questioned God on why Louis was in the family room with the children. God told me it was because Louis was the reason that John's family was going to heaven because Louis preached the gospel to his family and led them to the Lord. I shared the dream with John Jr., Renee (his wife), Louis, and Lynn. We all agreed that it was the sign that John would pass into heaven when he died. That day, we all went to the hospital because it was getting close to the hour that John would die. Louis and Renee left the room to go and grab something to eat. John Jr. was reading a book and Lynn was eating an egg (funny how one remembers such weird details). I was reading the Word of God over John to help him prepare to go home to the Lord. Suddenly, the atmosphere changed and the Holy Spirit entered the room. You could feel God walk in and suddenly, I could feel the presence of God and Jean. I could even smell her fragrance. Jean had died 11 years earlier, but she always wore a certain fragrance when she was alive. When the smell entered the room, I started crying and bolted out of the room into the hallway. Lynn came out and asked me what was wrong. I told her about what had happened and asked her if she could feel it. She told me she was too involved in eating her egg. When I re-entered the room, I asked John Jr. if he could feel what had happened. He responded, "You mean when Jean entered the room." He could feel it too. I do not believe there is Biblical scripture to back this up, but I believe that when one is dying, God opens up Heaven and prepares the dying loved one by bringing his or her loved ones to greet him or her as they pass from the Earth to Heaven. In addition, when the fragrance and the presence of God and Jean came into the room, John smiled and reached up toward the ceiling as if reaching for someone. Right after this happened, Louis and Renee came into the room. Louis told me that I needed to come and look at something. They led me down into the lobby, turned me around and told me to start walking and looking. As I did, Louis explained to me that the prophetic in the spiritual realm often manifested in the natural realm. I looked over to my right as we were walking, and there was a family room. In the family room was a fireplace mantle with wine color on the bottom and gold on the top. As we entered through the doorway there was a sign that read "Family Room." I started to cry and told them both that God had shown in the natural what I had dreamt (seen) in the spiritual. When we returned to John's room, we read some more of the Bible over him and told John Jr. and Lynn what had happened down in the lobby. We all agreed that God had solidified the answer to John going to heaven. A few days later, John died and entered into the glory of his heavenly home. John Jr. stated that he had died peacefully in his sleep. The mercy of God is there for every person. He exhausts all possible avenues to salvation because the Bible states, "The Lord is not slow in keeping his promise, as some understand slowness. Instead he is patient with you, not wanting anyone to perish, but everyone to come to repentance" (2 Peter 3:9). God reached forth to John unto the last moments of his life giving him every opportunity to accept Jesus as his Savior so that he could enter into eternal rest with the Lord. Praise God that John accepted the opportunity to receive Christ, even on his death bed!

Sadly enough, at the same time death found its way down to another state. We got a call that Louis' brother had a stroke and was lying in a hospital down south ready to die. So, we attended the funeral of John, only to get in a car with our children to drive thirty plus hours to a hospital to help Louis' brother die. When we got to the hospital, his brother was hooked up to an IV, had a feeding tube in his stomach, and was still receiving Dialysis. He could not eat or drink because his Esophagus was paralyzed from the stroke. After speaking to him about the Lord, Louis prayed with him and his brother decided that he was going to remove ALL life saving measures and all medications, inclusive of his Dialysis. His brother wrote a new health directive and had everything stopped. He requested his own beautiful "living wake" and got to say goodbye to all his friends and family. This was so beautiful. Everyone said kind words and sang songs to this dying man. He got to hear his own

Eulogy and enjoy the words that all would have said at his funeral. He also requested that Louis went to the nursing home in the next town where their sister was just admitted and was "failing" in her health. He begged Louis to make sure that she knew the Lord so that she could be in heaven. What one needs to understand, the previous year two other of Louis' brothers had died – one from a heart attack and the other from congestive heart disease. So this was a very sad and tragic time because we had just attended the funeral of his other brothers who had died the previous year. We made our way to the nursing home, prayed and sang with his sister, and then we started our way back home. On the second day of driving, we received word that Louis' brother died and passed into glory. The following year, his sister died and passed into glory. So, our family grieved three brothers and one sister in the course of three years. Each one received Christ before passing away. They were all in their early sixties – and little did we know that Louis would pass into glory the following year.

# CHAPTER III

# MIRACLES IN THE FIERY FURNACE

During the first seven years of marriage with Louis, we were not lacking in trials. During these fiery trials we felt like Shadrach, Meshach, and Abednego. This story from the Bible is about three young men who would not bow down to King Nebuchadnezzar, so they were thrown into a fiery furnace to be burned alive. The furnace was stoked seven times hotter, but when they got into the furnace there was a fourth man standing with them – King Nebuchadnezzar declared him to be the Son of Man – Jesus. When they walked out from the furnace the Bible says their clothing was not even singed nor did they smell of smoke; the king declared to the entire kingdom that Jesus was Lord and made a decree that all his subjects would bow to the one true living God. When these three men trusted in the Lord, He provided a miracle in that furnace for them. We found the same thing as we had our share of fiery trials; God provided miracles for us.

During all the various trials came various miracles. I could not possibly share them all because there are too many, but I will share a few stories so that you, the reader, can hear testimony of the faithfulness of God. The title of this book, *When All Hell Breaks Loose, Heaven Crashes In,* will come alive in the next few stories. When Faye was two years old, she broke her arm in half between the wrist and elbow, God crashed in as the mighty physician. Jeremiah 30:17 states, "For I will restore health to you, and I will heal you of your wounds, said the LORD . . ." This is just one of a plethora of verses about how God promises to heal you from sickness, disease, wounds (physical, emotional, spiritual, and mental), and a variety of other ailments. As the story goes, on a Tuesday afternoon a friend came out of my house screaming that Faye had seriously broken her arm. She explained that Faye had been on a rolling chair and fell off. Her arm was hanging in a "U-shape" from the elbow to the wrist. Louis and I rushed her to the emergency room where she was immediately given pain medicine and prepared for surgery. As we awaited surgery, we started to pray for a miracle. The Orthopedic surgeon did surgery on her arm by "reducing" it and putting on a cast up to the shoulder. He told us that she would have to wear the cast for at least 6-10 weeks and would most likely need physical therapy after that. We left the hospital on Wednesday afternoon. That evening, we took her to church and asked the church to pray for her arm. The pastor, elders, and members of the church prayed that she would be given new bones in her arm. Five days later, Monday, I had to take her back to see the same surgeon in order to make sure the bones had not moved. When I got there the x-ray technician asked me what had happened. I told her and then she took Faye to have her arm x-rayed. When she returned she stated, "I thought you told me that this little girl broke her arm?" She showed me the x-ray and told me that her arm had never been broken before. We were both amazed. I yelled out, "Well, Praise God." I knew God had answered the very prayer that the entire church had prayed. When we got in to see the surgeon, he confirmed what the x-ray technician had said. He showed me the before and after x-rays and stated that her bones had never been broken. He told me that if they had been, there would be white lines where the break had been, and there were not even white lines. He was so astounded he did not even know what to do. He stated that there was no reason to leave the cast on the little girl and he removed it and sent us home. God had taken what was a terrible situation and provided a way out and brought glory to His name! Bless the Lord!

Miracles continued to happen to help soften the blow of each trial that came. We were at church on Sunday when our daughter, Michaela, who was about two and a half, fell on a drumstick and it went through the roof of her mouth. It left a thumb size hole in the fleshy part of the top of her mouth and she was bleeding quite a lot and it had turned black and blue almost immediately. I put her in the car to go to the hospital. She was crying so loud; I asked her if she believed Jesus could heal her mouth. With her little girl faith she shook her head yes. As I drove, she and I prayed. She almost instantly stopped crying and told me all the pain had gone. I pulled over and looked in her mouth; the blood was completely gone, the bruising was gone, and the hole was completely gone. This little girl's roof of her mouth – completely restored. Praise the Lord!

At another point in time our daughter, Lynn (who was five years old at the time), was sitting in Sunday school and suddenly she could not breath. Her teacher came running over to me and told me that my daughter was turning blue and could not breathe. I asked what had happened and she stated that she did not know, she simply could not breathe. Louis and I started praying and put her in the car. All the way to the hospital we laid hands on her chest and prayed. As we prayed, she slowly started to be able to breathe. When we got to the hospital, they rushed her back and x-rayed her chest. The entire time her breathing kept getting better. When the doctor came with the x-rays, he showed Lynn the x-ray and explained to her that her chest had cracked and her lungs had started to collapse and she should have died. He then told her that it looked as if someone had glued her chest back together. He was utterly amazed and told her that she had a miracle. There was no apparent reason for our little girl's lungs to have collapsed. She did not get a blow to her chest or any other accident. We came to the conclusion the devil wanted to kill her, but the Lord intervened and another victory and miracle to the credit of God.

Another testimony of an astounding miracle was the day that Faye had a temperature of 106 degrees. I rushed her to the hospital because I couldn't get her temperature down. By the time I got there she was trembling. I was so afraid seizures would start. In the waiting room, I started to pray. Louis was at home praying with the other children. When they finally called me in, they gave Faye

Tylenol and Motrin at the same time hoping this would do the job. I was still praying (very loudly) as I walked the halls with her. I commanded her temperature to go down in Jesus' name. Within a minute of receiving medicine the temperature dropped to 104 degrees; the nurse was amazed. A minute or two later it went down to 101 degrees. The doctor was so astounded; he told us that he did not understand but that we could go home. Again the Lord had healed one of our sick children.

My oldest daughter, Jean, had contracted Lyme's Disease. Anyone who knows about this disease knows that over time it is crippling and deadly. After much prayer and two rounds of medicine she ended up back at the doctor sick again. This time they wanted to send her home with a month long permanent IV. We did not want this. We took her to church and went up for prayer. A lady with Lyme's Disease herself laid hands on Jean and prayed for her. Our daughter was instantly healed of the disease. We took her back to the doctor to have this confirmed. He told her she had a miracle. What I found so interesting: God healed our daughter, but the lady who prayed for her still had not been healed. The only possible way to explain this is that God decides who will be healed and who will not. The Bible states that healing is a free gift for all who ask, yet some do not get healed. I do not have an answer for this and neither does any other human being. All that we know is that God is in charge. Healing is accessible to all who have faith and will believe in the blood of Jesus and the atonement of the cross. This is where Jesus died and shed his blood that sickness and disease would be exchanged for healing. Some people would say that if God isn't going to heal all, then why bother to pray for healing. All I can offer as an answer, if you do not ask Him, how do you know if He is going to extend the miracle? The Bible states in James 4:2 "We have not because we ask not." So often, individuals do not receive healing because they do not bother to ask God. Does this stem from fear or disappointment of not receiving? Possibly. But I reason this way, what does one have to lose? If one asks, one may be surprised that God does a miraculous healing; if one asks and God does not heal that time, then one is no worse off than one was when one started the prayer.

The healing was not just confined to my immediate family. God released grace to even my extended family through me. One example of this was in my father. He was not a believer at the time of this miracle, but miracles are not confined to just believers. One can find many instances in the Bible when Jesus healed non-believers just because of the faith of others. One example is found in Mark 2:4 when a paralyzed man was healed. It was the faith of his four friends that allowed for this healing. They took him on his mat to Jesus (by breaking a hole through the roof and lowering him down no less), and when Jesus saw the faith of the four friends, he told the man his sins were forgiven and to take up his bed and walk. This same kind of faith was extended from me to God for my father. I received a phone call from my sister that my father had fallen off a roof (he was in his mid-seventies). Why he was on the roof to fix it at that age one will never know. The Lord had impressed on my heart to go and pray for my father. I felt the Lord tell me that He would heal him. I went to the hospital and was very shocked when my father allowed me to pray for him. His rib had broken in half from the fall and punctured a hole in his lung which was rapidly collapsing. I put my hand over the place where the hole was and asked "in the name of Jesus" for him to be healed. I left the hospital – not even sure if God had done anything. An hour later, I received a phone call telling me that my father was released and sent home. I found out that God had not only closed up the hole, but inflated his lung and put the rib back together. My mother was struggling to believe it and actually got angry because she had told everyone that God did not do "modern day" miracles and they were only for the Bible days. It did not matter though, God had done a great miracle and even the doctors acknowledged it and sent him home with that declaration.

This next testimony is not so much about healing as it is the faithfulness of God through a series of trials. "Both babies are fine." This was the statement that I heard on the other end of the phone that day. "Both! Did you say both?" was my response. I immediately started to cry. What you need to understand was that this pregnancy was bringing forth child number seven and eight. I was on two forms of birth control in order to prevent this. Louis was scheduled for a vasectomy but had to wait for six months after the birth of Faye. I had gone to the doctor to find out a sure way not to get pregnant again. He told me that he would put me on two forms of birth control so that if the first did not work, the second would. Lo and behold, I wound up with two babies instead of one. What I need to explain is that the Lord desired for this to happen. No matter what earthly method I tried, He would have His way in order to answer the prayer of a twelve year old boy. Louis became a Christian in Arizona in the middle of the desert when he was twelve years old. He said that he walked outside, looked out at the mountains and desert, and decided that there had to be a God. He was not raised in a Christian home, and God was never spoken of. He cried out to God and asked Jesus to be his Savior. He stated that He could feel the Holy Spirit enter into his heart and he stated that his chest started to burn. Well, somewhere out in that desert he prayed a prayer. He told the Lord he wanted to be just like his dad; he wanted eight kids with twins at the end. Louis was one of the twins (boy and girl). So here was the answer, about thirty two years after Louis' twelve year old prayer. He was about to have eight kids, twins at the end (boy and girl). Isn't that just amazing? Back to the original story: What overwhelmed me the most was that at the time I received this news I had a nine month old, an almost two year old, and a three year old. I would be bringing home twins in less than two months. There would be four babies in diapers and three that could not walk. I had three teenagers at the time who were thirteen, fourteen, and fifteen years old. I was home-schooling and doing daycare. This seemed absolutely insane and overwhelming to me. Louis was working graveyard shift and two jobs. I was pretty much a single mom. The doctor asked me what he could do to help. I remember laughing and saying, "What is it that you could possibly do? I will have five kids three and under and three teenagers." He did not know how to respond to me.

When the Lord had told me that I was going to have eight children, I argued with Him. God was about to honor Louis' prayer, and I did not want this. After six pregnancies, nine months of sickness with each one, and very hard labors, I wanted to be done. When I went on the two forms of birth control, I was sure we were going to be done. The Lord had other plans.

One night at a prayer meeting, the Lord told me he wanted me to have eight kids. I laughed and told him that I did not want to do that. The power of God came over me, and I fell to the floor. I was actually stuck there for two hours. The entire time the Lord was trying to get me to submit to him and say yes to having eight children. Finally, a word came forth from the pastor that someone at the prayer meeting needed to submit to the Lord. I knew that was me. When I finally told God "yes", I immediately was "unstuck" from the floor. Little did I know: I was already two weeks pregnant with twins. The following day, I was driving and the Lord told me that I was pregnant, and I needed to get a pregnancy test. I went into the doctor and had a test done. The doctor came out to tell me the test was negative and announced that I should be happy. I stated that I would be if it were true. When I left, the Lord spoke to me and said, "Whose report do you believe?" I answered, "Yours of course." He then told me that the doctor was wrong, and I was pregnant again. The following day, I was driving past a drug store, and the Lord told me to go in and buy a pregnancy test. Sure enough! It was positive. Then Lord then told me there was a baby boy inside of me and then told me what I was to name him. At that time I did not know there were twins. Right before the ultrasound at about seven months along, there was one week that I saw twins everywhere that I went. Each time I saw them, the Lord would speak to me and say, "That will be you." Then one morning that week, I broke open an egg with two yolks. Lynn, who was about 12 years old at the time, stated, "Mommy, that chicken would have had twins just like you are going to have twins." The phone call confirmed all these times. I called Louis crying so hard. No one could possibly understand how overwhelmed and scared I was.

Physically, my body got huge the last couple of months. I ended up going on bed rest at thirty weeks because the pressure of the babies had dilated me to four centimeters, so I had to quit my daycare job. No income was coming in, and we were about to live on Louis' income alone. Before I could even tell Louis that the doctor had put me on bed rest, he called and stated that he was coming home from work. He could not walk because his knees had inflamed. That did not make any sense; there had been nothing wrong with his knees. When he went to the doctor, he was told it was Bursitis that was causing the inflammation. Now here we were with no income at all. We decided that we would not fret and started to pray. All this took place on a Friday. We told no one the problem and just asked God for provision. That Sunday morning after church a couple came up to us. They told us that a few weeks earlier God had spoken to them in their prayer time and told them they would be giving us a large sum of money but that they would have to wait for the right timing. Then they told us that this morning was the time. This couple gave us enough money to pay for all our bills, groceries, gas and spending money for two months. It was close to $5000. They told us that it was a gift and we were not required to repay it. We were shocked and stunned. God had provision already there before the trial had even begun. God states in the Bible that the Body of Christ is His hands and feet. This was one time that we witnessed that very verse coming to pass. The Bible also states that we are not to worry about what we are to eat and drink. "Therefore I tell you, do not worry about your life, what you will eat or drink; or about your body, what you will wear. Is not life more than food and the body more than clothes?" (Matthew 6:25). Also, "Therefore do not worry about tomorrow, for tomorrow will worry about itself. Each day has enough trouble of its own" (Matthew 6:34). God already knows our needs and has provision for them even before we ask. One must put trust in our provider: Jehovah Jireh (God the Provider), the One who sees and knows.

One more recent miracle came in the form of a healing of my own soul. Earlier in the book, you read of how my father did not want me. I spoke of how I never heard the words "I love you" and was not shown affection. A short while ago there was an incident where I needed to forgive my father for some very evil words he had spoken to me. My parents were not in my life for about twenty years, and about seven years ago the Lord had me call them and try to start a relationship with them. To abbreviate a very long story, the relationship was there but strained, to say the least. During a recent conversation, my father started to scream at me and told me to "Go to hell" and get out of his life! This offended me so much because he knew that I was a Christian; I could not believe he would say such hurtful words. In my anger, I told him that he would never see me again. I told my only Christian sister of the scenario and declared to her that I was done trying to be their daughter. I was so tired of the emotional pain. Year after year it seemed to only get worse no matter how much I tried to love them. Then came the day God intervened and did a miracle. My father asked for a meeting with me. I could not figure out why, so I called my sister and asked her to come with me. I made a statement to her and it was this: "I will not ever speak to that man again until he apologizes to me for damning me to hell." One needs to understand the power of this statement. My father NEVER apologized to anyone in our lives. He never admitted he was wrong, so the chance of him doing this was "nil to none", as the saying goes. We did go to my parents' house and had a very stressful dinner. My parents did not speak to me the entire evening. Finally, in their living room my father brought up the fact that my son had gotten married and they were not told or invited. I tried to explain that I had nothing to do with that decision. The discussion got very heated and my father stood up and started screaming and swearing at me. I sat and let this happen well into an hour and never lost my cool. Finally, my father made a snide remark to me about why I was going to church if there was so much pain involved. He yelled at me and told me to stop going to church. I tried to explain that I did not want to stop going to church, but was having trouble trusting pastors because of all the pain over the years. Then he swore at me and told me to leave his [@# %&*^] house and never come back. I started yelling at him and told him that I would happily leave and never come back. I was crying uncontrollably as I screamed at him. In my yelling, I told him that he could never understand what I was feeling because his daughter had not been molested or impregnated by a married "holy" man. My parents knew of the tragedy of what happened to my young daughter. I ran into the bathroom and was crying and screaming because the emotional pain was unbearable. I could not see beyond my father's 'hatred' for me (at least that's what I thought). Little did I know that while I was in the bathroom, my sister was crying and asked my parents if the purpose of the meeting was to beat me emotionally further down than I already was? She explained later to me that my father dropped into his chair defeated and simply said, "No." When I came out, I sat down and turned my chair to the window and told my sister that I wanted to leave. Before I could get up, my father walked over to my chair and the most incredible thing happened; he very tenderly got down by my face and looked into my eyes and said, "Lily, I am sorry if my words have hurt you. I love you, and I want you." He turned and walked away. Then my mother walked over and told me that she loved me. I was so stunned and shocked that I could not even respond. These were words I could never remember hearing in my entire life. My sister got up and said through tears, "Lily, did you hear that? He apologized!" I simply nodded yes, and then I got up to leave. At the door my father hugged me and again told me he loved me. Immediately, years of pain and hurt dissolved. I was no longer angry and was able to completely forgive him at that moment. It was a true miracle of God – my father was "human." He admitted his sin, apologized, and I was healed. James 5:16 states, "Therefore confess your sins to each other and pray for each other so that you may be healed." God provided power in the act of confession of a sin and forgiveness. This was truly a miracle that I did not expect that day. Since then, my relationship with my parents has been completely different. Not perfect, but full of love and honor.

I could write page after page of miracles and wonders, but surely you, the reader, would become overwhelmed and exhausted to say the least. So, I will tell you a final story of a time that God provided healing for our little one. Grace, who was about ten months old, got a parasite in her intestines. They think it was because they gave her too strong of medicine for an ear infection. Anyway, she was being eaten away from the inside by this parasite. After about four months of fighting it, medicating her, and taking her for prayer numerous times, the doctors told me that they could not help her anymore and that she was going to die. The medicines for this were either too strong for a baby, or she was allergic and threw up continually. All of man's help was exhausted and they told me to take her home and just help her die. On my way to church, I was praying and crying, and I asked God if He was going to take my baby. I told Him that if He was going to do that, could he please prepare me. He gently spoke to my heart and said, "Will you give her to me?" I was weeping and responded back that I would because she ultimately belonged to Him, but that it would be very hard for me. The Lord then reminded me of something I had heard years earlier, "Hold things loosely in the palm of your hand so when the Lord needs to take them, He won't have to pry your finger off them." The Lord then said to me that I must hold my children loosely in my hand so that when He took them from me He wouldn't have to pry my fingers from them. I envisioned my hands opening with my children in them and I replied "Yes" to the Lord. I freely offered my daughter back and that very morning at church God healed our baby - miraculously and wonderfully healed. There was not a trace of the parasite left. This is how we knew she was healed. She had been having about twenty to thirty bowel movements per day and they were sticky, black, and looked like tar. When she ate, her food would immediately come out in chunks and then the rest of the bowel movements were the tar. I was going through about a bag of diapers a day. She was rapidly losing weight and was very pale. After being healed, she had a normal bowel movement. After that she started to gain weight and all went back to normal. The Lord be praised! Isaiah 53:5-6 states, "But He was pierced for our transgressions, He was crushed for our iniquities, the punishment that brought us peace was upon Him, and by His wounds we are healed." We had been watching this very promise fulfilled time and again in our life. The Lord wanted obedience during this trial; obedience to release our children's lives to Him. This was a test that I didn't realize later would come to pass in our life.

# CHAPTER IV

# AMAZING GRACE

December 10, 2000 was the fatal day where our trust and faith would be tested. In our lives, when the Lord required radical trust and faith, He always prepared us for the fiery trial. It was October 2000 when the Lord sounded the warning trumpet. In our life, it came in the form of Bible verses, dreams, and visions. Louis and I had been in prayer on this particular October evening; the Lord showed me a vision of Louis and me in a boat. There was a great storm blowing all around us but we were not being affected in any way. Then the Lord showed me a high cliff. In the cliff was a cave. I saw the hand of the Lord put a person into the cave and a great tidal wave started to come against the cliff. It was of hurricane magnitude. But what I saw was that the person in the cave was not being harmed in any way and was being cared for. I knew the person was me. Then the Lord spoke and told us that we were going to have a great storm come into our life. He assured us that we would be protected and cared for. The same time this was happening, the Lord spoke to my heart and told me that Louis would have a dream that night. Some important information about Louis is that he hardly ever dreamed. He had only a handful of prophetic dreams the entire time I was with him. I did not tell him what the Lord spoke to me. We ended our prayer and then went to sleep.

The following morning he woke and said to me, "I dreamed all night long." I chuckled and asked him what his dream was about. He told me that God sang a song to him all night from Psalm 46. It reads like this: "God is our refuge and God is our strength, a very present help in trouble. Therefore, I will not fear though the Earth be removed and though the mountains be carried into the midst of the sea." We decided we would stand upon this scripture no matter what came our way. If God was faithful enough to warn us about a great storm coming our way, then He would definitely be great in that storm. In addition, we definitely knew that if God said it would be GREAT, then GREAT it would be. Louis also told me that in his dream he heard three words. They were firstborn, in-laws, and visitation. He told me he did not exactly know what they meant but that he thought the first born meant that one of our firstborn would die, either Michaela (which was his firstborn) or Jean (which was my firstborn). The other two words (in-laws and visitation) did come to pass, but that is another story.

A short while after that, the Lord spoke to my heart and told me that Jean and her baby were going to die. That was so hard to hear, so I just pushed aside that thought. A couple of days later my sister called and told me that she had a dream that in the dream there was a tragedy and she thought that someone in my family was going to die. I quickly responded that it would be Jean and her baby because the Lord had already prepared me. Now it was beginning to sink in that this was really going to happen. At the time, I thought she would die in childbirth because of complications she had been having. I assumed she would hemorrhage to death and then the baby would die, but that was not how her death happened.

On Sunday, December 10, 2000 Jean's baby shower was scheduled at my Mother's home. At that time, my mother and I weren't exactly talking because of the religion issue. She just couldn't accept that I had given my life to the Lord and was not Catholic anymore. I chose to attend a different church. Despite that fact, I was scheduled to be at the baby shower. That morning when I woke up, the Lord spoke to me and told me that I could not attend the baby shower. I did not understand this at all. The Lord also told me that I could not take her sixteen year old sister with either. I questioned the Lord about this, but He simply told me I could not go. Later I realized this was God's hand in my life. I called Jean and told her that I would not be attending. She started crying and asked me why not. I did not have any great answer except that the Lord had spoken and told me not to go. I assured her I would be giving her the baby gift when I saw her next. We discussed having her grandmother cancel the shower because there was severe weather outside and driving warnings, and Jean had a long drive to her grandmother's house. She was living with her father at the time, and the two of them decided she would still go. The hard part was that she was on bed rest and was very sick. I again encouraged her to wait until after the baby was born (which was scheduled for only four days away) to have the shower. She stated the baby shower was already scheduled and she was going. I told her I had to obey God and stay home.

 I decided to go to the grocery store to buy Christmas dinner that we had scheduled early to have with Jean because her baby was to come that week. When I left home, Louis was with the five little kids at home. Lynn had gone with a friend shopping and John Jr. was with the youth group at church. While I was at the grocery store I kept thinking about Jean. For some reason, I couldn't get her off my mind, and I felt like something was wrong. A dreadful feeling hit my heart; it was a void and I knew that something was terribly wrong. I started to cry and pray for her and the baby. All the way home the feeling would not go away; in fact, it kept getting stronger. I asked the Lord what was wrong because I thought she might have gone into labor. When I arrived home, the house was bare. I thought this was strange, and I did not know where Louis was. I found out later he was called to work on an emergency and took all the little ones with him. I looked over and saw the phone blinking on the message machine. When I listened to the machine, there were seven messages. Seven! Wow, I never had that many messages. The first message was my mother, and she sounded very distraught. The message said that I needed to call her house immediately. I did not wait for the other six messages. I knew something tragic had happened to Jean and the baby because, remember, she was supposed to be at my parent's house for a baby shower. When I called my parent's house my sister answered the phone. All that she would tell me was that there had been a bad car accident and I needed to go to the hospital where they had taken Jean. The only thing I remember saying was, "Is my daughter dead?" She would not tell me; she just kept saying that I needed to go to the hospital. I just kept asking the same question: "Is Jean and the baby dead?" She still would not tell me. She told me that my friend would be there to watch the kids and that Louis would bring me there. I finally hung up and just waited. I did not need to be told, I knew that my daughter was dead. When one of your children dies, there is an unexplainable hole in your heart. That was what was wrong at the grocery store when I felt the void. There was a hole in my heart even then, where Jean resided. I later came to find out that at the precise moment I felt the void in my heart was the exact moment she died.

I immediately called the pastor to tell him that Jean had been in a bad car accident, and I did not know how badly she was hurt. He told me that he already knew. Apparently, one of the men at the church worked for my sister and she had called him to find out if he knew where I was. She told him what had happened and they told John Jr. who was at his house having youth group. He was already on his way home. I called the house where Lynn was supposed to be, but she was still out shopping. Later, the father of the girl that Lynn was with came over to see if he could help. He told me that he would keep trying to locate Lynn to tell her to go to the hospital.

This whole time I remember pacing the floors and frantically praying for Jean. While waiting for confirmation that she was dead, I kept praying for the Lord to keep her alive until I got to her so I could find out if she had given her life back to the Lord. She had been struggling terribly with her walk with the Lord. My friend finally showed up and started praying with me. Louis and John Jr. were still on their way (which seemed to take forever). I was frantically praying and rambling on to our two friends.

I was receiving constant phone calls from my sisters asking me if I was on my way. I kept telling them that I was waiting for Louis. Finally the confirmation phone call came. I had a sister, Rae, who had given her life to the Lord earlier that year. We had become good friends, but she lived out of state. She had been struggling with Laryngitis, so what she had to say got blurted out with no warning. She pushed out her words and said, "It's a God thing, Jean and the baby are dead!" I remember thinking, "How can that be a God thing?" She did not mean the fact that they were dead, but the fact that I was still at home for her to call me and tell me the news. After Rae got "saved" her relationship became very strained with the family (as did mine), so when she called the hospital to talk with them, they would not tell her anything going on. When she called the nurse's desk to inquire about her niece, the nurse answered and simply stated that Jean and the baby had died. This was so strange because news like that is never delivered over the phone. That was part of the "God thing." The nurse also told her I was already on the way to the hospital. So, when Rae called and I was at home, she stated that it was a "God thing" referring to me being home so that she could deliver the news and not our parents. This would explain why Louis got delayed and took so long to get home. Even for bad weather conditions, I seemed to wait for an eternity for him. The way I responded to the news probably would have gotten me a straight-jacket (or sedated at the least). The Lord knew where I needed to be in order to receive this news. In addition, He had my dearest friend with me to lean on. Louis being late also allowed me time to prepare myself to go to the hospital which was about forty minutes north of where I lived.

My reaction? Good question! When Rae blurted out the news, I fell prostrate upon the floor. The phone was still in my hand, but I was no longer talking to my sister. I was now talking to the Lord. I was yelling to (not at) God. I was not angry with Him, but I needed to remind Him of all the promises He gave to me about my children and eternity. He had made numerous promises to me over the years that my children would be in heaven with him. I reminded Him particularly of the ones in Proverbs 22:6, "Train up a child in the way he should go, and when he is old he will not depart from it," and Jeremiah 31:16, "But now this is what the LORD says: 'Do not weep any longer, for I will reward you,' says the LORD. 'Your children will come back to you from the distant land of the enemy.'" From what I could tell, Jean was probably not going to have eternity with God because she was willfully sinning. The Word states in Hebrews 10:26-27, "If we deliberately keep on sinning after we have received the knowledge of the truth, no sacrifice for sins is left, but only a fearful expectation of judgment and of raging fire that will consume the enemies of God." Jean was willfully sinning every day with her boyfriend and was deliberately ignoring the truth of the Word of God, but I knew what the Lord had promised me. So, I began to petition the Lord with my request: "If she is in heaven, you can have her, but if she is not in heaven, I need her back so she can get saved." I told the Lord I was going to lay hands on her and raise her from the dead so His promise could be kept. I knew God could not lie, so I told Him I needed an answer about where she was. I could not accept the fact that she was not with the Lord.

Most people would probably think that I was too bold with God. To be honest, I may have been, but to be told your first born daughter is dead and to know she is in heaven is one thing, but to be told that she is dead and not know if she is in heaven is a whole different story. I was frantic, devastated, confused, and the grief was overwhelming. The whole time I was ranting to God, my friends just sat there and prayed and cried with me. Louis finally got home. I remember falling upon him and sobbing. I had been frantically pacing before he got there, continually reminding God of all His promises. I continued to do this while we waited for John Jr. and the five little ones. Louis had met up with John Jr. and gave the kids to him so that he could bring them home. While we waited, I informed Louis that we would be raising Jean from the dead if she wasn't in heaven. I told him the same thing I had told God. If Jean was in heaven, God could keep her, but if not, He had to give her back so she could be saved. I made mention earlier of a time when God had asked me to hold loosely to my children so when He took them He wouldn't have to pry my fingers off them. Well, the time had come to give her over; I was willing to do that if she was with the Lord. I knew this was a test, and I needed to pass it. So, not only did the trust start, but a time of testing to see if we would praise the Lord even when He took from us one of the most precious gifts he had ever given us, our first born child, Jean. Not only did she have to go but also our firstborn grandson.

We called the pastor to tell him Jean had died and asked him to meet us at the hospital; he agreed that he would come with his wife. In addition, I told him the same thing that I had told God and Louis. He did not argue and agreed to help us pray for the raising up of Jean from the dead. After the children arrived with John Jr., we told them Jean had been in a bad car accident, but we did not tell them she was dead. We prayed with them before we left so that they could trust Jesus to take care of everything. John Jr. was coming shortly after we left because a sitter would be arriving soon. He was coming up with my friend. It was now three o'clock in the afternoon; Jean and the baby had died around 1:30 p.m. On the way to the hospital, I was so numb I could hardly think. I remember opening the Bible to 1 Kings 17:21-22 where Elijah was staying in the home of a widow. Her son died and he raised that son from the dead by stretching himself upon the boy three times saying, "O Lord my God, I pray, let this child's soul come back to him." I felt faith rise up in me when I read this. I did not know if Jean would rise up or not, but I do know the Lord brought that scripture to me for one purpose and one purpose only – to boost my faith, so when I had to lay hands upon Jean I would not doubt for one moment that she would rise up from the dead if the Lord so willed it.

When we arrived at the hospital quite a scene awaited us. The first people we met were my parents. They took us into a conference room with the doctor and a priest. I was so numb that I just stared straight ahead. I do not even know where Louis was at that moment. My mother simply said to me, "It is obvious you already know that Jean and the baby are dead. Who told you?" I responded to her by saying that I just knew and no one had to tell me. I did not want to get Rae in any more trouble than she was already in with our parents, so I kept silent.

I was escorted to the room where Jean and the baby were. I remember Louis coming over to me, and I grabbed onto him. When we rounded a corner I saw Jean's boyfriend, the babies' father, sobbing on the shoulder of his friend. I cannot even express all the feelings going through me now. I did not even like this young man. He, not only, took my daughter from me and refused to let her have a relationship with me, but he verbally abused her and controlled her every move. I did not know how to respond to him. The Lord had to do work in that area. I found myself gently reaching over to touch his shoulder. He turned and saw me standing there, and I did not expect what happened next. He fell at my feet and started to sob. He told me that he was sorry that he ever took Jean from me and asked if I could ever forgive him. He repented for all the trouble he had caused and said he did not mean to and did not want things to turn out this way. What do you do when a very broken, grieved man repents to you? Of course, I forgave him. I simply told him to get up from the floor and that it was water under the bridge and that it did not matter at this point. I took his hand to go see Jean. He had not seen her as of yet.

When we reached the door to the room, my knees went totally weak and started to buckle underneath me. I had never, and I mean never, seen a freshly dead body before. I had only seen dead people in coffins after being embalmed. Louis caught hold of me and my dad told me to take slow even breaths so I would not hyperventilate. When I saw her, I cannot tell you how absolutely sad I was. Her baby was lying on top of her, and they were both lying there white and dead.

Before I go on, let me take you back to when the car accident happened and how the story was relayed to me about the situation. As I said before, Jean was on her way to her baby shower at my parents' house. As she was approaching their driveway she lost control of her car when she was turning into the driveway. The roads were very slippery that day, and the car started spinning a 360 degree circle as it slid on the ice and went into the other lane. Her car was struck on the passenger side and was badly crushed. The other car had two passengers, a 22-year-old man and a 15-year-old girl. Both passengers were hurt very badly and were flown to two different hospitals in St. Paul and Minneapolis. Jean was dead on impact. Her head trauma was severe, and her neck was broken in half. Her lungs had collapsed, her main artery in her heart was torn out, and all her organs were split and damaged. You probably did not want to hear all this, but I wanted to give you an accurate picture of how great an impact her car took. I thank God she died instantly because if not, she would have been a "vegetable" because of the brain damage and the broken neck. I would not have ever wanted to make decisions like putting her in a skilled nursing facility or unplugging life support. I believe God's hand was on her that day. Even though she was dead on impact, they continued to give her CPR to try and save the baby. When her car was hit in front of my parents' house, the family came out to help. They did not know it was Jean in the car because they did not know the kind of car she drove. It was when one of my sisters went to see who was in the car that she came face to face with Jean. She started screaming that it was Jean. I was told my oldest sister, who happens to be an RN, did CPR on Jean until the ambulance got there. My father fell to the ground crying, and my mother and aunt started praying the "Our Father." I cannot imagine the trauma to my family after having seen the accident happen and knowing this was their granddaughter and niece. I am sure that for a long time to come they will have images in their minds they would rather not have. As I stated before, the hand of God was on Lynn and I because we were not at the baby shower and did not experience this traumatic scene. The Lord knew Jean would be killed that day, and we probably could not have handled seeing the car accident. I thank God that even hard situations, like not getting to attend your daughter's baby shower, are turned for the good.

When the ambulance took Jean to the hospital they did an emergency Cesarean to try and save the baby. They were not able to because he had bleeding on his brain from head trauma, his liver tore in half, and he had bleeding in his stomach. He died a few minutes after the Cesarean. He was a very beautiful baby who weighed about 5 ½ pounds and was 18 inches long. He looked just like Jean; he was so precious - an absolute doll. So, the only time I got to hold my very first grandchild was when he was dead. From the moment of hearing about Jean's death to the bitter end of everything, we knew and could feel the awesome grace of God as He walked with us. "His grace is sufficient" took on a completely new meaning. Just the fact that He gave us strength to go to the hospital and endure the events there was simply amazing.

Back to the hospital story; when I saw Jean and the baby laying there my heart exploded in grief. I remember sobbing for a long time on top of her and touching the baby a lot. I kissed them what seemed like a hundred times. I knew they would soon come and take them away for the preparation process. Shortly after seeing them, the coroner took me into the hall and talked with me about Jean and organ donation. The baby could not have his organs donated because he was one week too young. He needed to be thirty six weeks along in the womb, and he was short of that by a few days. I consented to let them take from Jean whatever they could use. They took Jean's eyes, bone marrow, muscles, and skin. They used these for cancer patients, burn victims, blind patients, and so forth. Jean had always told me that she wanted to be a donor when she died. A few weeks after her death I got a letter telling me that her eyes were used to help two cataract patients and one blind individual; each got the needed parts to help them see again. Even her death brought incredible blessings to people.

After I left the coroner, I was taken back to see Jean again. I remember feeling like a robot. There was so much numbness and shock. The pastor and his wife arrived shortly after that, and I went out to meet them. I took the pastor and his wife in to see Jean where everyone else was assembled. After a short time, I made everyone leave; I only kept Louis, the pastor, and his wife with me in the room. We proceeded to pray life into Jean. I reminded the Lord that if she was in heaven, He could keep her but otherwise she needed to rise up. I stretched myself out upon her dead body three times, breathed into her mouth, and spoke life into her. This was how I felt the Lord was leading after reading 1 Kings about the child raised from the dead. If faith alone could have raised her from the dead, Jean surely would have risen that second. I had faith that could have moved one hundred mountains. When she did not rise up, I spoke to the Lord and stated, "Okay God, she did not come back, so I assume she is with you. Now you need to let me know for sure." Over the next four days, the Lord started to reveal to us that Jean was with Him in heaven. John Jr. and my friend arrived shortly after the scenario of prayer; I stood with John Jr. as he grieved. I continued to inquire about Lynn because she still had not arrived. John, Jean's dad, was now standing at the head of Jean's bed. He was another person I had to face. I had not seen or spoke with him since he had taken Jean to live with him. John Jr. and Lynn had not seen him that whole time either. They both decided when John moved Jean's boyfriend into the house with Jean, that he was helping her ruin her life so they refused to see him or speak to him. This time was equally hard for the two of them. Lynn finally arrived. I remember her coming down the hall and just falling on me. She could not believe her sister was dead. Lynn fell completely apart when she saw Jean. She was sobbing so hard that she fell to the ground at the head of the bed. I just cried with her because I did not know what to do or say. I remember committing both Lynn and John Jr. into the hands of the Lord. Lynn grieved so hard, not only had her sister died, but her best friend. She was devastated. The grief in the room was overwhelming. The Word of God promises help in times of grief, "As a mother comforts her child, so will I comfort you," says the Lord. (Isaiah 66:13). "But you, O God, do see trouble and grief; you consider it to take it in hand. The victim commits himself to you; you are the helper of the fatherless" (Psalm 10:14). These are just two of many different promises of helping those in grief. I knew the Lord would be there for us all.

After grieving with everyone for a while, I asked to be alone with Jean one last time. Out of desperation, I laid hands on her again and started to speak life into her. I said the funniest prayer over her. It went like this: "Jean, I know your spirit can hear me, so if you are in heaven you can stay there. I would never want you to leave such a beautiful place. But, if you are not there, (I just could not force myself to say the word Hell, even though I knew it was the only other option), get your butt back in this body and come to life." I guess one never knows what one will say in desperation and grief. Oh well, God honors prayer no matter how confused and sad one is. Anyway, Jean did not come back to life, so more than ever I was convinced she was in heaven; I just needed confirmation and God was faithful to give confirmation.

After walking out of the room, I had to deal with John and funeral preparations. He wanted to take Jean up to Pine City where she had been living and bury her there. I told him absolutely not. I reminded him I had raised her by myself for sixteen years and her home was in St. Paul and that was where she would be buried. After all, I told him she was mine and that he had not helped raise her at all, and I still had full custody of her. I made sure he knew that I would decide where she would be buried. I was hoping the Lord would intervene and make John compliant this one time – and He did.  John did not argue with me and her boyfriend told me that whatever I wanted he would do because I was Jean's mom.

I remember having all kinds of feelings that were not right, and I had to let God deal with them.  I tried so hard to keep my mouth shut because I did not want to hurt John, but at one point I did break down.  It was when we were discussing what funeral home to contact for the funeral arrangements.  All of the sudden grief overwhelmed me, and I fell to the floor with my face against the wall.  I was not really talking to anyone at the time, so I simply stated to the wall, "If John wouldn't have taken her from me she would still be alive.  He destroys everything he touches."  I continued to reiterate, to the wall, all that had happened since she had left home.  I did not really think about the fact that he might have been listening to all of this.  I remember when it was all over he simply touched my shoulder and said he was sorry.  I could not accept that at this time even though I knew I had to forgive him and let it all go.  Over time, I was able to do this.  Right at that moment, God needed to soothe my heart before I could get to the place of forgiveness once again.  He did this over the next few days, and I was able to be kind to him and pray for healing of his heart.  Before we left the hospital, John told me that he loved me. I was not sure how to react to this. I simply patted his back because there were no words. I did not know what to say to this person who had spent so many years trying to destroy me. Only God knew!

I still had the dilemma on how to figure out if Jean was in heaven. I was impatient on this one, so before her boyfriend left I went up to him and pulled him aside to ask him the question: "I need to know, did Jean love Jesus?" I was shocked by his statement and did not seem to fully understand it. He told me that Jean loved Jesus with her whole heart, mind, and soul. In addition, he told me that on Friday, Jean told him that she and the baby were going to go to heaven when they died, and he needed to love Jesus like she did so that he could be there with them when he died. That seemed a strange way to preach to someone, but my question was answered; she loved Jesus. It seemed very strange to me that she had mentioned dying to her boyfriend. The Lord had begun to confirm that she was in heaven, because on Monday, the day after her death, I received a phone call from my younger sister, Lee. Jean and she were good friends. Lee started out the conversation with, "I have something I need to share with you." She proceeded to tell me that on Thursday morning Jean called her to tell her a dream that she had had the night before. In her dream she stated that her baby had died, but she was not at the funeral. She then told my sister that God appeared in her dream and told her that she and her baby were going to die that week. God also told her that she needed to wake up and give her life back to Him because it was time to come home. This would have explained why on Friday, she told her boyfriend that her and the baby were going to die, and he needed to 'get saved' so that he would be in heaven with them. God was so faithful to Jean, because He forewarned her and prepared her to die. I believe that God is faithful to the end of one's life and will fulfill His promise of salvation to those that have accepted and believed in Him (even when one of His sheep stumble and fall). The Bible states, ". . . My sheep hear my voice, and I know them, and they follow me. I give them eternal life, and they will never perish, and no one will snatch them out of my hand. My Father, who has given them to me, is greater than all, and no one is able to snatch them out of the Father's hand. I and the Father are one" (John 10:26-30). The one thing I continued to reiterate to all my children was that they needed to LOVE JESUS! If one loves Jesus, I believe He will be faithful to save and deliver from all sins and shortcomings. Once one has given over his or her life, Jesus will be faithful to do the rest. Philippians 1:6 states, "And I am certain that God, who began the good work within you, will continue his work until it is finally finished on the day when Christ Jesus returns." The promise of the good work of salvation will be completed when one loves Jesus and continues to walk with Him.

When I left the hospital I felt much lighter and was not so downcast. Louis and I knew that the Lord was walking through the grief with us while answering all the questions. The Bible says that He is near to the broken hearted. We were definitely broken hearted, and we could feel the Lord drawing near to us. In fact, He was carrying us. The Lord showed me that He carried those that were going through hard trials. That night I did not sleep. I kept seeing Jean over and over again. I saw her in heaven with a white dress on. It looked like a cotton dress that hung to the floor. It was quite a simple dress, but beautiful. I saw her pushing a stroller. I kept seeing her look back at me and tell me that she loved me. Then, I saw her pick up the baby and take him to the bank of a river and sit with him in her lap. This vision went on for hours. I remember hearing the Lord sing to me the words to the song, If *You Could See Me Now.* The words went like this:

> If you could see me now, I'm walking streets
> of gold, if you could see me now; I'm standing
> tall and whole. If you could see me now,
> you'd know I've seen His face. If you could see
> me now, you'd know the pain's erased. You
> wouldn't want me to ever leave this place,
> if you could only see me now.

I chose this song for her funeral; I wanted everyone to hear this song, so they could realize that Jean and her baby were with Jesus. Through the night, I could not stop thinking about her. I got up and started to talk with the Lord. I told Him that I needed to know for sure that Jean was with Him. I knew he had done so much already, but this is what else I said to the Lord. I began to tell Him that I was in so much grief I could not decipher what was His Spirit and what was just wishful thinking. I could not really decipher if the visions were from Him or from me. I told the Lord that the only thing I knew to be true was His word and could He please use it to show me Jean was with Him. I started to frantically flip through the Bible. I did not know where to turn or what scripture would speak to me. All of the sudden, I stopped in the book of Psalms. I can't begin to tell you which one, but I know this much, my eyes fell upon one sentence. It said, "Though they sinned, yet were they saved." At that instant, peace flooded my soul, and I knew that I knew Jean was with Jesus. It was a peace that surpassed all understanding. My heart knew! But as faithful as God is, He did not stop there with the confirmations.

Over the course of the next three days there were four different people who told me that God had revealed to them something about Jean. All four of these people told me this at different times and did not know the other ones said the same thing. These individuals shared that God told them that out of His sovereignty He took Jean home. He explained to them that if she would have stayed upon this Earth any longer, the devil would have gotten her soul. She would have gone to hell. You see, Jean was such a gentle soul, and her boyfriend and dad were abusing her. I do not believe that she could have remained firm in her beliefs with such abuse happening. Later in the week, God confirmed to me what the four people had told me. He reminded me of Isaiah 42:3, "A bruised reed I will not break and a dimly burning wick I will not extinguish." I remembered talking with Jean shortly before she died and remembered something she said to me. Jean told me that she did not want me to give up hope on her. She told me that she had a flicker of light left in her, and I needed to keep praying for her. Finally, the Lord spoke to me and said, "I did not allow the world to break this bruised reed or extinguish Jean's flickering flame. I brought her home so this could not happen." I clung to this promise and rejoiced in what the Lord had revealed to me. The Lord began to answer questions I did not even ask. He was revealing His purposes for having her leave this Earth.

As I sat through the night trying desperately to make sense of the day, I was sobbing by my stereo. I was crying to the Lord telling Him I was sure that this grief was too much for me to bear. I begged Him to help me and give me strength. Everyone in the house was still in their rooms; I am assuming the kids were asleep because they were up much later than normal the night before. After we told the kids Jean had died with her baby they cried for a long time. We prayed and just held them before they could fall asleep. In those wee hours of the morning the Lord began to minister to me. He began giving me strength that I would need to get through the next three grueling days. First, the Lord spoke to me and told me I was not walking this trial, but He was carrying me. The strangest thing happened next; I felt my body being picked up and come off the ground. For the next four days, I did not feel the ground beneath my feet. The Lord was actually carrying me at a time of incredible grief. Have you ever read the poem, *Footprints in the Sand?* It is a poem about a man who gets to look back at his life. He notices two sets of footprints as he walks through life. When he sees the parts of his life when he had troubles he notices there is only one set of footprints. The man questions God about why there was only one set of footprints at the lowest times in his life? The Lord answers him and states that it was at those times that He carried him. I suddenly felt as if this poem had come to life in my situation. After that, the Lord laid a song on my heart: *Jehovah Shalom, Jesus is our Peace.* The peace of God overtook me and flooded my heart. Some of the words that ministered deeply: "Peace when trouble flows, Jehovah sees, Jehovah knows. He is our peace, when trials near, Jehovah sees, Jehovah hears." As I listened, the words of this song assured me that not only does God see, but He also knows the sorrow and pain we bear. The Lord continued to amaze me into the morning hours. God placed a burden on my heart to pray for all the people who were grieving because of the deaths of Jean and her baby. It was amazing how as I prayed, my own grief was comforted even more. This reminds me of the verse, "He comforts us in all our troubles so that we can comfort others. When they are troubled, we will be able to give them the same comfort God has given us." As time went on, I was able to comfort others with the same comfort I received on this wonderful night of grief. During my prayer time for all the hurting people, God gave me a vision. I had been praying for ministering angels (like the ones who came to Jesus when He was in the wilderness for 40 days and the devil came to tempt Him) to come down and comfort all the people who were hurting. God opened up the heavenly realm and showed me Jean's car accident as it was happening. He showed me the two angels that took Jean and her baby to heaven. As I was watching this happen, I saw a multitude of angels coming down and start going to all the different people who were grieving. The Lord whispered to me that He was dispatching angels down before the accident ever happened. The angels were preparing to go to each individual who was going to be affected by the horrible car accident. In addition, He told me He has a special army of angels that He only uses during times of tragedy on Earth.

It is the job of these angels to go and comfort those who are grieving. He sends one, two, or more angels to each person and sends them according to the amount of grief they are suffering. This was a truly amazing vision and revelation. Then a thought occurred to me, "Why should this surprise me so much, when I know our God is sovereign and merciful?" He loves us so much, and He shares in our grief. He is the great comforter and can comfort us in a way that no one else can.

After spending time at the feet of Jesus receiving comfort, I got up. When the children went to bed, as I stated earlier, they were all crying. One of the things Michaela, our seven year old, said was that she wanted to hold the baby. I tried to explain to her that she would not be able to because when she saw him, he would be in the coffin and she could not remove him. She fell asleep crying very hard. That morning, she came bounding down the stairs very happy and lighthearted. I was surprised and asked her why she was so happy. She relayed an amazing story to me. She told me that she prayed that Jesus would let her hold Jean's baby. Then, she shared that Jesus appeared to her with Jean and the baby. She said that Jesus laid Michael, the baby, in her arms and let her hold him. She even described the baby in great detail; amazingly it was completely accurate of Michael when we saw him at the hospital. She talked of his soft, light brown hair, and how warm he was. Then she said Jesus told her they had to go and they left. I was amazed at how God took care of the grief of that little girl by actually appearing to her and granting her the one request she had. He is truly the one who comforts in times of grief.

On Monday, my sister, Rae, came to stay at the house. We had so many things to do in the next few days. Louis and I had to meet with the funeral director to start the funeral arrangements. All these things were done in a mechanical motion. When people experience such a loss, everything that needs to be done is performed in a state of numb. God was still working and did another amazing thing when my sister arrived at my house. She had laryngitis and could hardly speak a word and over the next six days she ran my house. There were seven kids in the house under the age of seven years old. Her patience never ran thin and she was able to take care of all the kids and household items. In addition, over that time period and the following two weeks, the churches Louis and I had attended in previous years brought meals to us. The people at his work brought food and so did the owner of the corner store. I assure anyone who thinks the Body of Christ is not at work, they are wrong. We experienced an abundance of love from the Body of Christ during this time. The church responded with love by becoming the "hands and feet" of Christ.

Louis, Lynn, John Jr., John, Jean's boyfriend, the pastor, his wife, and I all met at the funeral home to get things started. All the details take a very long time. We had to arrange the entire funeral inclusive of songs, speakers, pallbearers, and more. I had never buried anyone before, so this was really hard for me. There were so many decisions to make, and they took most of the day. I thank God for our pastor and his wife. Without them, I don't know how any of us would have finished this process. They were there to help make decisions we couldn't make or didn't know how to make.

The following day brought more decisions. We had to choose the mortuary. We had to find a place to bury Jean. We ended up choosing a mausoleum at the request of John. It was extremely difficult to pick out a head stone for Jean. It sure helps to set the reality and the finality of death. It seems when you feel you have no more strength left; the Lord gives more and one is able to go forward. At this time we felt an extreme measure of grace poured out by the Lord. He continued to carry us through.

Now the COFFIN! What a word. This was the most difficult task of all. We all walked into the room to look. Images flashed through my head while standing there looking at these coffins. I kept seeing Jean and Michael lying in one. It was so strange. Her boyfriend could not go on. He had to leave the room. Grief overwhelmed him, so Louis and the pastor went out to be with him. When I arrived outside to check on them, I came upon a beautiful sight. Louis and the pastor were praying the salvation prayer with him. I was astonished! Compassion for this young man overwhelmed me. I walked up to him and out of my mouth came words that only God could have placed there. I told him that if Jean's death resulted in his salvation, then it was not in vain and worth it. The Holy Spirit had to have done a work for me to acknowledge any of this. The Lord showed me that a life for a life was exactly what Jesus had done on the cross. He had died that we all could live eternally with God. This is what had happened as far as I could tell. Jean's death resulted in her boyfriend's eternal life. This was something I could rejoice in and could again see a glimpse of the purposes of God. More comfort came to me. The Word of God states that all heaven rejoices when a sinner comes home. I was imagining at that moment Jean having a party with the angels. As you can recall, she preached to him before she died and told him that he needed to "get saved" so he could be in heaven with her and the baby, and that was happening right then and there.

That night Jean's boyfriend wanted to come and have Christmas with us. He wanted to give to us the presents that Jean had for us. He came and gave us the gifts. A few months prior to Christmas, Jean told me that she wanted to make the kids each a quilt for their beds. Once I saw the gifts, I couldn't fathom how she had time to make all the quilts. God had used the precious time she had left upon this Earth to leave each of us with a wonderful gift of love. He even knew what would bring comfort from such a tragedy in our lives. She had chosen a material that fit each of the children's personalities, and one that would match my room. Each child got a twin size quilt, and Louis and I got a double quilt. It was quite a miracle that she got these done considering she was seventeen, pregnant, and very sick. She finished nine quilts in less than three months' time. AMAZING! John Jr.'s quilt had wild game on it because he loves hunting. Lynn's quilt was made with bright yellow sunflowers; she loved yellow. The five little ones all got cute little animals to fit their personalities. Louis and I got a patchwork quilt with roses the exact colors of our bedroom. God had used Jean to give us each a precious gift that was made with extreme love. A love covering for our beds to remind us of Jean; that was what I thought the quilts represented. God even used Christmas presents to bring comfort to us all – may His name be praised!

We thought we would have a morning of rest before the wake but this did not happen. That morning we had to finalize details, and we had many people calling us. I don't think our phone stopped ringing for three days. The messages just kept piling up. I did not have the energy to call people back; we got the children dressed and were on our way to the wake before we knew it.

The time came for us to view Jean and the baby before all the people arrived. My children, John and Jean's boyfriend, his mother, Louis and I were all in the room. In the beginning, Grace, my five year old, couldn't bear to see her. She stood in the bathroom with her hands over her ears and just screamed. Louis finally went in and talked to her because when I tried, it was no use. Louis helped

Grace write a love note to Jean. Grace later told me that she was afraid of what Jean would look like. Earlier, the kids had all drawn pictures and when we got there they all placed them in her coffin. There were so many little kids' pictures that we hardly had room for them all. Jean had many cousins who were very small and loved her a lot. They had all made her some sort of a drawing. Our youngest son, who is a pretty laid back, quiet kid, did something that was unusual for him. When he saw Jean, he ran over to the couch and in anger he tore the couch apart; he flopped onto it in complete sadness. There my three year old lay. It is so astounding to see the different ways in which small children react to death. His twin sister could not stop kissing Jean and the baby. The other three kept touching Jean, kissing her, and telling her how much they loved her and how much they missed her. This was a picture to behold. God was amongst all these little ones. Over the course of the night we watched Him comfort each of them so that the acceptance of this tragedy would become reality to them. Lynn and John Jr. simply cried a lot. Then it was time to open the doors.

 The amount of people that flooded through the doors was startling. For three and a half hours the stream of people was nonstop bringing well wishes and sympathies. I was amazed at the supernatural strength that was bestowed on Louis and me. John Jr. was doing the greeting and was being a fine young man. Lynn was desperately trying to hold herself together. She did a great job until she had enough and fell apart. Someone came to get me to help her. By the time I got to Lynn she was sobbing at the foot of the picture boards we had made. All she said was, "Mommy, I wish that everyone hated Jean and then we could all go home." I knew she did not mean this, but I realized that she was so overwhelmed by the amount of people; there were over five hundred or so people that walked through the door that night. Louis spent all his time proclaiming the goodness of God, as did I. We both told all those we came in contact with how blessed we were. This was true – not a show. We were experiencing the grace of God and seeing the fruit of God in this terrible tragedy. What the devil means for bad, God changes to good. We watched so many lives touched and hearts changed as they were witnessing the grace and goodness of God. We continually stated that God was good all the time – not just in good situations, but also in the bad. One thing we had learned over time was that one could not look at circumstances. God is a never changing God and was still wonderful no matter what the circumstances. It did not matter if the fire was burning hotter as tragedy hit. Louis made a statement at the funeral where he stated, "we are not overcome by grief but we are overcome by the grace of God." We knew this to be truth because we were in the midst of enormous amounts of grace. People came to us so stunned because of what they saw God doing. They could not understand this peace in a time of great tragedy. They were seeing us bury two people we loved and yet there was peace. We knew that only God could give such supernatural peace – this is what we shared.

One particular woman was amazed by this. She shared that she had buried her husband, sister, and brother all in just a short time. She simply could not understand how we could declare that God was so good. After talking with her, we hoped she would see the blessing in such a tragedy. Another woman, who I knew was a woman who had much trouble accepting the turn of events in life, was simply overcome with amazement. She said, "Wow, I can't believe you two are at such peace and are smiling." Another couple came up to us and told us they were blessed by us because in a time when we should be the ones being ministered to, we were ministering to others. We could only glorify God and declare that it was all in His hands. It was not in us at all to do this; it was the working of the Holy Spirit during this time. The list of testimonies of individuals who were touched during this time is very long, but it was definitely time to close the doors and go home.

By this time I was going on four nights of no sleep and minimal food. I had lost at least ten pounds. The incredible thing was that I was still going. I do not believe it was adrenaline alone, but the amazing grace of God. I was still floating, and I can tell you my feet had not been on the ground from the beginning. The Lord continued to carry me as He had promised He would do.

By now it was Thursday morning and time for the funeral. I had not slept again. I was at home with all the children and Louis. My sister had gone to a friend's house to spend the night. I could not face my responsibilities when morning came. I was extremely sad. I had hit the point in grief where I was asking the "what-ifs?" to God. I walked into the bathroom and sunk to the floor. Tears flooded from me. I kept thinking about if I had been a good enough mom; was I too hard on Jean, what if I said anything that hurt her deeply, did I tell her I loved her enough, and so forth? I was consumed by a deep hole in my heart that was threatening to suffocate me.  At that moment the Lord showed forth His compassion once again.  He allowed Jean to appear to me.  I saw her standing in a white gown, and she told me that I had been a good mom.  She told me I had done my job well and that she was in heaven because of everything I had taught her.  She told me not to worry because she was where she was supposed to be.  She told me she loved me and was gone.  This put my questions to rest.

I often tell other people to "get up and brush off" when stupid mistakes are made in their lives, and that is what I needed to do.  I got up, brushed off, and dressed my kids and fed them.  To me, this was a great accomplishment that morning.  I was not dressed at this point because I could not face the funeral.  I did not know how to bury my first-born daughter and grandson.  Then another disaster happened; John Jr., who grieving himself, started to badger me.  He followed me around the house asking me why the kids weren't in dresses.  My answer was simple – they did not have clean tights.  I did not really care at this point.  I was just happy they were dressed and fed.  Then he started to "carry on" about me not wearing a dress because I had put on pants.  It was very cold outside that day.  Then it happened – I snapped!! He told me that if I wore pants to his funeral, he would kick me out. I started to scream at him. I told him I did not care. I was crying so hard and was so sad! After a lot of words he got angry. He slammed the bathroom mirror so hard that it broke. He started out the door screaming that he just wanted everything to be perfect. I ranted about how things were not perfect; I was burying my daughter and grandson today. By this time my sister came in the door. She said the Lord had put urgency upon her heart to get to my house. She came into this scene. I was hysterically crying by the mirror rambling about the grief in my heart, and John Jr. was on his way out the door to leave. Louis was trying to keep everything under control, but when a whole house is grieving it seems as if all things were out of control.

    It was five minutes before a limo was to pick us up, and I was not even ready. I quickly picked out a skirt and blouse, for John Jr.'s sake, and put it on. I finished getting ready and then we left. All the way to the church I felt numb. I stared blankly ahead crying, asking the Lord how I was to do this very hard thing. I was worried about John Jr. who had left in his own car. I prayed for him and his safety and placed him in the Lord's hands. I knew all that had happened earlier was simply grief. Lynn and I held hands as we drove to the church. When we arrived there were so many people. I remember telling Jean's boyfriend I could not handle one more person telling me they were sorry. I knew they all meant well, but I was overwhelmed with grief. A friend of mine was there, and I went up to her and relayed the story of the morning. She listened and then quoted Philippians 4:13 to me where it says, "I can do all things through Christ who strengthens me." I felt the Spirit of God well up inside of me and fill me with strength in every part. I looked at her and told her she was right and that I could do this. First point of action, to find John Jr. When I located him, I apologized for the morning and told him I loved him very much, He and I hugged, and then I marched up to the front of the church to stand by the coffin and continue to greet the many people who came to view Jean before the funeral – then came time for the funeral service.

It started with the closing of the coffin. I did not find this to be so hard. I kissed Jean and the baby one last time and said my goodbyes. I knew that this was just the shell of a body that used to hold Jean's spirit. When I came to this realization, it was much easier to watch the casket close. Lynn, John, and Jean's boyfriend had a much harder time.  Louis, John Jr. and the five little ones were okay up to this point.  I went over to Lynn and told her to pull herself together because she had to sing.  Lynn and her friend sang a new song named "Peace."  Lynn had to then give the Eulogy.  She had never done this before, yet she did a wonderful job.  Many people came up to talk about Jean and many wonderful things were said.  When all the people were done speaking, Louis and I went up to speak.  God gave us such strength to do this.  When I turned around to speak, I was stunned.  Then church was full and there were about 2000 people present. WOW!!!! I was astonished.  You never know during your life time how many individuals you touch through ministry until they all gather in one spot to show love and support.  Louis and I stood and proclaimed God's goodness.  We told the people how blessed and overwhelmed by God's grace and goodness we were.  I quoted Job, which later became the title to my first book.  I stated that even in the midst of the tragic death of our daughter and grandson, we would still praise our Lord.  This alone changed many hearts and lives. After we had worshipped and watched a video of Jean during her life, the funeral ended and we took the casket to the burial place.  I remember leaving the coffin there and saying, "It is finished." When I turned, God took a very large portion of grief from my heart. This was the beginning of healing.

The testimonies starting coming in from those who offered feedback of all the things God did at the funeral. It was incredible. We know that we probably only heard a small portion of what happened to people, yet we were still amazed. Here are some of the testimonies: A lady at the home-school co-op where I attended shared with me that the morning of the funeral God spoke to her heart and told her to come. She was not going to go because she had only met me once. She had just started co-op and did not know very many people. She told me that she had to give a message on the faithfulness of God that Sunday at her church. She stated that God had taken her into the book of Job to the verse that said, "Though He slay me, yet shall I trust Him." She relayed to me that she did not understand it very well because she had never experienced this kind of faithfulness. It was then that God spoke to her and told her to come to the funeral. In addition, He flashed a picture of me before her eyes and told her that I was Jean's mother. She said she came and this is what she witnessed. She saw worship happening in the midst of great sorrow. She saw words of kindness spoken about

Jean. It was when Louis and I got up to speak that she said she froze in her seat because she could not believe what she was hearing. I quoted the very verse in Job that she was about to preach on. She stated at that very moment she understood the scripture verse and saw it in action. She went on to tell me that on her way home she called many others to tell them about the funeral. She said she had never seen a funeral like Jean's before. On the following Sunday morning, she told me that she had given a very effective sermon on the faithfulness of God during trials. She shared about Jean and her baby's funeral and then had an altar call for people to give their lives to Christ or renew their lives. She stated that every single person in the church went forward and lives were incredibly changed.

Another testimony from a lady was about Lynn. She stated that when Lynn gave the Eulogy about Jean and made a comment about Jean's one weakness, God started to minister to her. Lynn stated that Jean's one weakness was that she was weak. She made reference to the fact that Jean was weak and had a hard time standing up for herself. She commented that this weakness was also her greatest strength. Because of it, she was able to love anyone because she always saw the good in other people and was never unkind to others.

She stated that Jean always showed gentleness. When Lynn made this comment, the lady told her that it ministered to her. This woman told Lynn she struggled with people like Jean. Individuals like her never seemed to get mad and were always kind and loving. She did not like that they were weak. She shared about when Lynn gave her Eulogy; God ministered to her and gave her a love in her heart that day to love weaker people. She also shared that the Lord had her read an article about spiritually weak people and how important it was to love them. I guess we never know how God will use a situation to help people with their attitudes and draw them closer to Him and His ways.

The final testimonies I will share (though I heard there were many more) are about my own extended family. They have a bias opinion against pastors and born-again Christians. They call them "holy-rollers." Firstly, during the funeral, I was worshipping up front with my hands lifted and felt an urge to dance around. The Lord spoke to my heart and told me to stand still. Suddenly, I felt someone behind me grab hold of my waist. Immediately, I felt the Lord's presence and what felt like power leave my body. The scripture story about the woman with the issue of blood went through my mind. In that story, Jesus asked who touched Him. His disciples found this to be odd because there were many touching Him. Finally, Jesus stated that He felt power leave Him. That is when the woman admitted it was her, and she was healed. After the funeral, I asked my sister who touched me, and she stated it was my mother. I told her what happened and told her that I was sure my mother had felt it too. She went on to tell me that Mom had commented on that very thing and wanted to know how I could be so at peace and thanking God during the death of my daughter and grandson. Secondly, when the funeral was over my parents went up to John Jr. and told him that our pastor was very kind and gentle and they truly liked him. They told him they would listen to this pastor speak anytime – amazing! My father also told the pastor that it was a beautiful funeral and that his message was very good. This is quite shocking since the message was a salvation message. This was our request so that everyone in attendance would have an opportunity to hear the gospel and respond to it once in their lifetime. I found that God could even reach the hearts of people who are biased against Christians and soften their hard hearts during crisis.

When we arrived home, I found that life was very numb. Trudging through day after day of sorrow began to get old. There were so many children that were grieving; I found I did not even have time to grieve on my own. Little did I know, around the corner was to come many more trials as my oldest son, John Jr., got ready to leave for the Marines. Lynn fell into a deep pit of sorrow, depression, and destruction. I remember listening to a song called *Mercy Came Running*, and in this song there is a line that says, "When I couldn't reach mercy, mercy came running to me." This proved to be a true statement in our lives. When the times of intense grief and troubling behavior hit, God would come running with open arms and His mercy would prevail.

# CHAPTER V

# THE AFTERMATH: DRUGS, SEX, AND WAR

One would think the death of a child was the worst trial anyone could walk through. Possibly, but then more pain and overwhelming things began to happen. For whatever reason, God only knows, the Lord allowed storms to start plummeting our family. During a storm, when one hears thunder, right around the corner seems to be lightning striking. The rumbling of thunder began in our lives in every possible area: emotional, spiritual, physical, mental, and even financial. It is funny how God uses people and prophecy to help one understand that sometimes He allows trials to refine and purify one's life. Over the course of the next fifteen years there would be numerous people that made the statement to me, "Your life is just like Job in the Bible." "Job is written all over your life." Christian after Christian would walk up to me, and God would have statements like these come out of their mouths. Many of them, I never met before. Some, I knew, and they were aware of my life situations.

Some were my friends delivering a Word from God. All I know is that whenever I would start to wonder if I was doing something wrong in the sight of God, someone would approach me and tell me that God had sent them, and they would tell me that God sent them to deliver a word of encouragement to me. These words would always involve Job from the Bible. If you, the reader, have never read the book of Job from the Bible, I encourage you to open it up and sit back for an amazing story. This story is of a mighty and righteous man of God that the Devil sought to destroy. The Devil appeared before God with the intent of seeking Job's life. He brought accusations to God against Job declaring that the only reason Job worshipped and loved God was because he had a blessed life. God told the Devil that Job would love and worship Him no matter what, so God gave the Devil permission to do whatever he desired to Job, but could not kill him. The Devil began to plummet Job's life. This came in the form of his children all being killed at once, his wife divorcing him after telling him to curse God (when he would not, she divorced him), his animals all got sick and died, he got horrible boils all over his body, and finally, his friends accused him of sinning and told him that God was judging him. Through this entire scenario, Job never cursed God or stopped loving Him. In the end, Job passed the test of sifting from Satan, and God restored two-fold all that was taken from Him. God assured me that I had not sinned and that Satan was allowed to sift my life in order for God to show the devil that my family would survive. God spoke to my heart through these individuals and told me that I would pass the tests and all that was taken would be restored. The sifting began shortly after Jean's death.

During the times of grief, God continued to do miraculous things for us and other individuals. Often, I would feel the presence of Jean or would be allowed to see a vision of her. In addition, over time God continued to allow us the privilege of hearing stories of different people and how they were ministered to through Jean's death and funeral. The children's grief became like a consuming fire in the house. Louis continued to declare the goodness of God, but the problem with this is that he never allowed himself to grieve Jean. Twelve years after her death, he finally let out the pain. As I mentioned earlier, Jean's birth father had died of cancer. At his funeral, my family and I ended up going to the Mausoleum where Jean was buried. Her dad was going to be buried in the same wall.

This was overwhelmingly difficult. Having to see the grave site brought forth new and refreshed grief feelings. Everyone in my family was crying so hard. After the service was over, everyone started leaving, but Louis leaned against Jean's headstone and wailed at the top of his lungs. I believe all the years of grief for her came gushing out of him. This incident helped to bring our family and marriage to a place of healing. So to continue on, the children all grieved heavily after Jean's death. It took months for us to return to home-schooling and to any kind of normal schedule. From January to April there was so much to be done, yet I continued to walk through life just numb. Lynn crashed into a dark place and would not get out of bed. In January, I enrolled her in public school and to this day I often think I made a mistake, but it was the only thing I could think of at that time that would get her up and moving. While attending school, she hooked up with the "druggy" crowd and started to take Cocaine. She ended up giving sex to men in order to pay for drugs. All this craziness was heightened by five little ones who were just extremely sad. One night, I remember lying in bed crying, and Louis started to reprimand me for grieving. He accused me of not thinking God was good because I was sad. This incident (along with others) started many years of a troubled marriage.

Finally, the fatal day came, April 10, 2001. This was the day John Jr. was to leave for the Marines. When the Officer came to pick him up, the sadness overwhelmed me. Letting my 17 year old son leave was an extremely hard task. When goodbyes were said, he got in the car and as soon as the vehicle rounded the corner, I fell to my knees and broke down hysterically sobbing. This was my second child to be taken away. At the end of that day, Lynn fell apart. She had already been struggling, but when John Jr. left, she became violent and angry. She yelled at me and stated that both of her siblings were taken away from her, and she was the only one left. That evening, she started throwing me around and beat me up. At midnight, I called my sister (who had offered her a place to stay) and relinquished her over. As I watched her leave, I again hysterically cried. This was the third child to leave my life. I dove into a deep well of grief. For seven days I could not get out of bed, nor could I take care of my other five children. Finally, on the seventh day I said to the Lord, "I cannot live this way. How will I ever minister to another person when I can't even get out of bed to take care of my own children?" Then I asked the Lord to please take away the intense grief. An amazing miracle happened at that moment. I saw a vision (similar to a movie on a screen) of a person running a race, breaking the ribbon, and winning a prize. Then I heard the Lord ask me a question: "Lily, if your child ran a race, broke the ribbon, and won a prize would you cry and tell them to go back to the beginning?" I answered the Lord: "Of course not, Lord." Then He spoke to me again and said, "That is all that has happened. Jean ran the race of life, broke the ribbon which was her death, and won the prize of heaven." Then the Lord declared very definite to me, "REJOICE, MY DAUGHTER." As soon as He said this, the deep grief busted out of my heart and from that day forward I did not intensely grieve her anymore. Don't get me wrong, I often missed her and still do to this day, but I did not deeply pine and hurt over her. Isaiah 53:4 states, "Surely he hath borne our griefs, and carried our sorrows: yet we did esteem him stricken, smitten of God, and afflicted." God is faithful to bear our sorrows and griefs. He not only bears them, but He also walks through them with us.

Now came the time to walk through a son at war and a daughter who was engulfed in a world of drugs and sex. All the while these trials happened, Louis dove into a deep world of disappointment and discouragement as God allowed our ministry to crash and burn while Christians betrayed and hurt us. Our marriage became deeply troubled as our children struggled through life trying to survive each coming tragedy and sorrow.

Bit by bit, Lynn walked through her own world of destruction. From April until October, she filled her body with alcohol, cigarettes, Cocaine, and other drugs. She slept in the street for a few weeks and finally ended up living with the biggest Cocaine dealer in the Metro area. Lynn once told me that when her sister died, she died emotionally and spiritually as well. In my first book, Lynn wrote a chapter in the book that contained her story. I will share parts of this story with you. Prior to leaving home in April, Lynn stated that she became very depressed. Throughout January she tried to kill herself various times. She stated that various times she tried to end her life the same way Jean died. She would drive extremely fast on icy roads and then slam on her brakes. Each time, God would protect her car. He would always slide her over to the side of the road and nothing would happen. Lynn stated there were numerous other ways she tried to kill herself, but none of them would ever work. During this time, I was praying each day that God would protect Lynn and not allow her to die because she was angry with God. I assumed she would probably die unsaved, so I begged God to spare her life. Remember, God promised in His Word He would not break a bruised reed. At this time, Lynn was definitely as bruised as she could get.

Lynn continued to share her story by stating that April 10$^{th}$ she ran away from home and went to her Aunt's house. "At my aunt's house there was no love, no God, and I was in complete darkness. I felt like I had no one." She continued to share that she had her mom, whom she was angry with and did not want, and she felt as if God had abandoned her. As she relays her tragic story, you, the reader, can feel the depth of her sorrow. Jean and Lynn were best friends and did everything in life together. She felt as if part of her was ripped away. "Around June I felt like life wasn't worth living, and I did not care at all. I started to do every drug I could possibly get my hands on," states Lynn. She shared that she started dating drug dealers, so the drugs would be free. She found herself in horrible situations, was raped multiple times, physically and emotionally abused by the people she hung around with. Another miracle Lynn shared was how when she snorted Cocaine with her friends, they all developed holes in their noses that would bleed. She declared that God protected her nose from holes or bleeding even as she did much more Cocaine than the others.

Lynn continues her story by stating that her days were piddled away at her Aunt's house and at night she would sneak away to party well into the wee hours of the morning. She would sneak back into her Aunt's house only to start the whole routine again. "I wouldn't eat or sleep for long periods of time, stated Lynn. Once I went for thirty days without eating or sleeping. I lost about 15 pounds on a body that only weighed 115 pounds." During this time, God had instructed me to write Lynn letters filled only with blessings and scripture. At the end of each letter, I would always sign, "I Love You, Mom." Lynn remembers it this way: "Throughout this time, I would receive letters from my Mom. She would send me blessings in the mail. They were letters that would speak life into me and into my situation. These letters contained scripture and prayers. The letters also told me how much my mom loved me and was praying for me. At the time I wanted to hate it. I wanted her to stop praying for me and quit sending me letters; although, at the time it was the only thing that kept me alive. I finally decided, I did not want to hurt my brothers, sisters, or my parents any more so I decided to kill myself," remembers Lynn. She states that she hated herself and her life. She declared that there was no possible way she could pull herself out of her pit. "All I did was cry. During the day' I cried as I piddled my day away, and at night when everyone was passed out at the parties I would cry."

Lynn shares the glorious miracle that God did for her in the next part of her story. On the night she decided to kill herself, she was crying hysterically hugging her sister's teddy bear. She shares about how she cried out to God and told him that He needed to pull her out of this pit if He wanted her to live and stay on the Earth. She then shares God's process of salvation and deliverance. "He sent me a dream," declares Lynn.

> *"I was on a ship and there was a terrible storm like a tornado. Every time it would hit the boat, I would fall down and then I would get back up. This happened about twenty times. The whole time this was happening, I kept calling out for my Mom. Finally, I got off the ship and ran outside to get in my car. I started to drive, as I continued to call out for my mom. I started to look for her. I was screaming her name but could not find her. Finally, I hit a flood, and I could not drive anymore, so I got out of my car. I started to run the opposite way, the way I had just come from. Finally, I fell to the ground next to a girl. I looked up and the sky had split open, and Jesus was descending. I could feel Him in my dream, but all I could*

*hear was someone wailing and crying. The person did not want to go to hell, even though this person was proclaiming Him to be Lord. I could not decide if it was me or this girl who was screaming."*

"When I awoke," shared Lynn, "I told my Mom the dream. God had given my mom the gift of interpretation of dreams, so she shared with me the interpretation. The interpretation was this: The dream was my life. The flood represented my drugs and the storm represented Jean's death. When I was looking for Mom, it was because I knew she represented the only source of help for me, which was Jesus Christ. Yet, I felt so overwhelmed by the tragedies that I could not find help. When I fell down it was in total weakness; I could go no further. The voice screaming and wailing was the fear of me going to hell. Not knowing if it was me or the girl, was the confusion I felt over the fact that I was not positive of my salvation. Then, the proclamation of Jesus being Lord was the assurance that I was alright, and God was there to help me. The Lord split the sky and showed me Jesus, so I knew I was going to heaven. After the dream, the Lord provided a way to get me back home."

Lynn had her ups and downs the first few weeks at home, but finally, God completely delivered her from drugs, she gave her life back to Jesus Christ, and continued her journey forward through life.

One would have thought our family would have come to a place where the trials would have become less frequent, but the opposite seemed to be true. As time went on, each individual in the family had to walk through his or her own trials. Others in the family helped as best we could, but prayer is really the best way to help when others are suffering. The Word of God states that we should mourn and laugh with others, and one can do this, but what it all boils down to is taking the individual(s) to the throne room of God.

The day Lynn ran away to her aunt's house, an Officer came and took John Jr. off to the Marines. Little did I know, after boot camp, he would be going to Japan and finally end up in Iraq at war. After I wrote the first book (which was shortly after Jean's death), I met a woman who would help me get it into print. This woman, Renee, would eventually become John Jr.'s wife. After I had written the manuscript for the first book, I was given a name of a woman who helped individuals get their books into print. It was written on a very small piece of paper which I put in the bottom of an envelope and then forgot about it. An entire year went by before the Lord instructed me to contact the woman and put the manuscript into her hands to have edited and in print. The Lord gave me a dream and in the dream reminded me of where I had put the number to the woman. When I awoke, I went right to where the piece of paper was and called Renee. I spoke with her about the manuscript and what had happened (Jean's death) and informed her of how good God had been to us. She was so shocked because she stated that she had asked the Lord to put a "radical" Christian into her path – and boy! Here I was! I think I was a little more than she bargained for. Anyway, I met with her at a church, and when I walked into the door she was sitting on a bench. The Lord spoke to my heart and told me that she was going to be my daughter-in-law. I found this hard to believe, so I told the Lord that this was impossible because John Jr. was all the way in Japan. As far as I was concerned, they would never meet. I kept this piece of information to myself. I often spoke of Renee to John Jr., but I always referred to her as the "book lady." He did not know her name and a year later when he returned home from Japan, he came to church with us and by happenstance met Renee. Renee and I had set up a meeting in order for me to pick up the first 100 copies of my book. No one really called her Renee, they called her Reeny. I asked John Jr. if he wanted to meet the "book lady." He told me he did, and when I went to introduce them, he was shocked to learn that her name was Renee. To make a long story short, after we went home, John Jr. said he knew she was going to be his wife and when they first met there was a tug on his heart toward her. He stated that God had tugged his heart and told him she was to be his wife. Then, he told me quite an interesting story. He said when it was time to leave Japan, he saw a guy that he had not seen in a whole year. As they were talking, the man said to him, "so, you're going home to marry Renee, huh?" John Jr. declared that he did not know what he was talking about because he did not know any one by the name of Renee. John Jr. said that this man and he argued for quite a spell about this. "That was so strange," was John Jr.'s remark to me when he was relaying the story. After feeling the tug in his heart about marrying her, he thought her name was Reeny. He did not know her name was Renee, so when he found this out he was so shocked. As they dated and decided to get married, I confirmed to them that I thought they were to marry; I told them the story about God telling me Renee would be my daughter-in-law. The plans were that they would marry after a year of dating. Six months later, plans changed. John Jr. got his notice that he was to go to Iraq. Renee and he decided to marry immediately. Instead of the military chapel, the cell phone store where Renee worked became a chapel. They exchanged her use of the store for publicity. The local TV channel came and covered the wedding and the quick seven day plans. The flower shop down the street from where she worked donated flowers; the music store up the street donated the music. The wedding was beautiful and then came time for the send-off. There were so many tears. Who would have ever thought that John Jr. would end up in the war! It was the first initial battle to start the Iraq war. A year of bullets, bombings, and death as John Jr. walked out his trial. A year of worry, tears, and prayers as the rest of us walked out the trial half way across the globe. Renee moved in with us during that time. The days crept by as we sat not knowing if we would see John Jr. again. Mornings and evenings were spent in prayer as I lifted John Jr. to the Lord. Protection, peace, comfort, and any other prayer I could think of would be spoken to the Lord. There were a couple of times the Lord specifically woke me up and told me to prayer protection for John Jr. The stories he relayed of the protection of God on those days will always remind me of how faithful our God is. The Word of God states, "The prayer of a righteous person is powerful and effective" (James 5:16). I was counting on this and the Lord pulled through. Two different stories I will share with you so that the glory of God can be revealed through John Jr.'s walk in the war. One story, as relayed to me by John Jr., was about when his friends and he were under an open garage fixing their light armored vehicles. He stated that the "insurgents" (bad guys) drove by and opened fire on them. He stated that he watched their bullets in slow motion come at him and go around his head. It happened to be one of the very days the Lord woke me to pray protection. How incredible!!! The other story was also when the Lord had prompted me to pray protection because John Jr. stated that his vehicle he was driving rolled over a land mine. The mine blew and the only thing that happened to him was that he hit his head and sustained a "brain bruise" and a couple blown back discs. He stated that he should have been dead because that is what happens when you blow up in a land mine. God had again answered prayer and protected him.

When the year was over, John Jr. came home. He was a very changed man, but still alive. Renee and he struggled for the following ten years. Finally, they ended their marriage in divorce. This was very tragic for our family. The strain of John Jr.'s angry behavior, infidelity, and Renee's slobbish housekeeping, and refusal to have children or spend time with John Jr. ended their years of marriage. God was faithful to heal both of their hearts and put their lives back together. John Jr. is remarried with a new wife, new baby, and new business; Renee has moved forward in her job, life, and new marriage. Praise God that He is faithful even when we are weak and fail. The Bible says in Philippians 1:6, "For I am confident of this very thing, that He who began a good work in you will perfect it until the day of Christ Jesus." I continue to pray each day for all my children, in-laws (ex or current) and grandchildren that God will perform Philippians 1:6 in their lives.

# CHAPTER VI

# WITCHCRAFT (YIKES)

Prayer for my children seemed to increase in intensity as their life choices created a whirlwind of pain and suffering. What can you do as a parent when you see your children walking paths of destruction? I found that prayer and lots of unconditional love was the only way I knew to respond. God makes sure that we know in His Word that nothing can separate us from His love. Romans 8:35 states, "Can anything ever separate us from Christ's love? Does it mean He no longer loves us if we have trouble or calamity, or are persecuted, or hungry, or destitute, or in danger, or threatened with death?" He loves us unconditionally, but His love comes in all forms and discipline is one of them. "For the LORD disciplines those He loves, and He punishes each one He accepts as his child" (Hebrews 12:6). If your own father did not discipline you when you strayed away, what kind of a father would that be? It would be a neglectful one, I think. That is exactly what the Lord does when we need disciplined, He loves us enough to do so. There have been times I have experienced this kind of love from God, as have my children. God's discipline comes in various forms – a couple of examples: adverse consequences for sin, or turning one over to their own "stupidity" and allowing an individual to sink to the lowest pit (the only way out is to look up). Psalm 121:1 states, "I will lift up my eyes to the hills; from where shall my help come? My help comes from the LORD, Who made heaven and earth.…" Many times when one hits the lowest point of life after many bad choices, one must look up! A couple of my children have sunk pretty low. I continue to pray that when they are down, they will look up so that God can pull them up.

As a woman who raised her children to be Christians, one of the worst events that can happen is for one or more to walk away from the Lord. Lynn has not only walked away from God, but renounced her Savior, Jesus Christ. The day this happened, it ripped at my heart, and I bitterly wept. After much heartache in her life, Lynn could not accept that God was still a loving and good God. Her sister dying was extremely hard for her, but when her biological father, John, died, this was her demise. She fell completely to pieces and stood in my living room and declared that God had taken from her everything she had ever loved. She then renounced Christ and stated that God was not real. I begged her not to do this, but she could not hear my words. The pain in her heart was so deep. John Jr. and she had gotten into an enormous argument after their father had died. The argument was over money and his estate. John Jr. declared to me that she was not his sister anymore – they have ceased to speak for nearly six years now. Lynn had already tried to separate herself from all of us (her family) by taking her daughter and moving away. She got angry one day because she felt we were replacing her when we adopted a teenage girl. She stormed out and told me I would never see my granddaughter again. She stayed away for five years, but then with much prayer, the Lord brought her back. She had another baby, a son, by then and so she returned with her family a couple of months before her father died. I saw her once (at Christmas) and then her father got sick in April and died. After the argument between her brother and she, screaming and swearing she declared that we would not ever see her again. She left my house that day as I was begging her not to leave angry again. She did not seem to care and a couple more years passed before I got to hear from her again. One miracle that I would like to share: right before her father died, Lynn suddenly contacted me and told me that she wanted to have a relationship. I cried so hard because this was an answer to many years of prayer. She sent the children to come and visit for two weeks during Christmas time and this was very shocking. I did not realize how deeply her and her husband had sunk into drugs and witchcraft. When the kids arrived, they started to share about all the demons they saw and that talked to them. They shared some very devastating instances that went on in their home for many years. They had seen much violence between Lynn and her husband, and they witnessed sexual acts that no two little children should have ever seen. But God was on the job! They were driving to Minnesota with their father and his friend. Early that morning the Lord had prompted me to pray for their safety on the trip. On the way to our house, the two men were drunk and were driving. My granddaughter shared a story with me the night she arrived. We started to talk about her name and she asked where it had come from. I explained that her mother, Lynn, had given it to her out of the Bible. She was astounded and started to tell me that she remembered going to Sunday school as a little girl (they had not been to church in approximately five years at that time). She went on to tell me that she remembered what she was told in Sunday school about Jesus and God. She said that her mother had told her that Jesus was propaganda bull (*&$#). She had told my two grandchildren that God was not real and just a made up fairy tale. To go on, my granddaughter shared with me that on the way to our house, her father and friend were drunk and had taken drugs. They were driving through the mountains when their car went over the mountain side. She said that an angel showed up and blew "fairy dust" (that's what she called it) on her and then caught the car and set it back on the mountain road. In addition, she stated that the angel had told her to believe in God because He was real. I was so blessed to hear that story; I had been praying for many years that God would make Himself real to my grandchildren no matter what they were being taught. He seemed to be right on the job. During the two weeks the children stayed with me, my granddaughter said the salvation prayer and declared Jesus as her Savior. BLESS GOD! There are no other words than that. The Bible declares that God desires no one to perish, but all to come to the knowledge of Him and be saved. 2 Peter 3:9 states, "The Lord is not slack concerning his promise, as some men count slackness; but is longsuffering toward us, not willing that any should perish, but that all should come to repentance". He had kept His promise to me and was beginning to save my grandchildren. Lynn became very angry when she found out that I had spoken with the children about the Lord and again declared I would not get to see my grandchildren. I began to pray again, and God reversed this decision one more time.

Interestingly enough, the next time I heard from her was when her step-father, Louis, got sick. She called after hearing he was diagnosed with Leukemia. Louis' funeral came and went and Lynn could not afford to come, so we did not see her then. It was after a few months that I decided to take a trip to her home state with my children, son-in-law, and a friend of Seth's to see Lynn and my grandkids. When we got there, I was shocked when I walked into her house. There were many different types of witchcraft items along with many different forms of "demonic" art. I do not use this term lightly because it was some of the scariest things possible. She had black magic books, intention cards (these are used to curse individuals), crystals, bones, and various other types of witchcraft apparatus. We had to sleep in her house one night and it was awful. There were dark spirits flying around and lots of moaning and tormenting noises. It was so bad, that Nicole hopped into my bed afraid and asked me to get the demons to stop. I simply commanded them in "Jesus' name" to shut up and go to the corner and stay there. It got quiet and we all fell asleep. There were many other instances where I came in contact with Lynn's witchcraft, but it was when my granddaughter told me that "my mama goes outside on a full moon and calls the dark spirits into her" that I realized how deep into darkness and truly lost Lynn was.

Around October 2014, Lynn called me and asked me to take temporary guardianship of her children. This was a true miracle from God, because she had declared I would not get to see my grandchildren again. The Lord had answered prayers and came to the rescue once again. During the next four months, my grandchildren began to pray with me, listen to the Bible, and finally one Sunday they decided to let Jesus be their Savior and both of them got water baptized. A very interesting thing happened the Sunday after they were baptized. A missionary from Africa came and spoke. He gave a testimony about a little girl whose mother was a witch and when she became a Christian, she had to deal with her mother's witchcraft. Finally, her mother came to know the Lord and burned all her witchcraft books. My granddaughter sat riveted to her chair as the man shared the testimony. Finally, she came to me and stated that the same thing had happened to that little girl as to her. She asked me if her mom could be saved like that little girl's mom who did witchcraft. I gave her an absolute, YES, and then we continued to pray for Lynn. Since this time, my grandchildren have gone back to California. I am not sure what has happened to them, but I continue to pray that the Lord will keep their salvation firm and protect them always. They continue to have a hard life; their father has been to prison and back for selling drugs. At this point, their mother, Lynn, continues in witchcraft, but does have a new fiancé and a good job. These two grandkids still deal with many trials, but if there is one thing I know is that no matter what happens, God will keep their salvation and will do what is best for my two grandchildren. In John 10:28 the Word of God states, "I give them eternal life, and they shall never perish; no one will snatch them out of my hand." I believe this with my whole heart, nothing anyone can do will take those two little ones out of God's hands where He placed them when they decided to love Jesus. My granddaughter has since text me how she still sees angels and one night there was one singing to her in her bedroom. The funny thing was that earlier that day I had prayed that the Lord would send angels into their rooms to help keep them while they slept. Another answered prayer as God proved His faithfulness once again.

Since Lynn is still involved in witchcraft (I haven't heard any different), I continue to believe God for her return to the Lord and expect to see her raising her family up in the Lord. The Lord still loves her and her children because the Word of God says this: "For I am convinced that neither death nor life, neither angels nor demons, neither the present nor the future, nor any powers, neither height nor depth, nor anything else in all creation, will be able to separate us from the love of God that is in Christ Jesus our Lord" (Romans 8: 38-39). In this scripture verse it states that neither angels nor demons can separate one from the love of God that is in Christ. Lynn has lost her way, but I believe God will draw her back to Him because He loves her and her family. I would encourage you, the reader, if you have walked away from the Lord for any reason at all, ask forgiveness and return to Him for He is waiting with open arms to receive you back. He is a forgiving and loving God who desires to walk through life with you and receive you into heaven on the day you die.

While praying daily for my wayward children, Louis and I fought our own battles and demons through life. The struggles became so hard and unbearable that our marriage began to suffer along with the spiritual walks of the children and Louis. I fought my own battles as menopause hit hard and dissatisfaction and depression seemed to want to engulf my life. Louis started to deal with failing health issues as he walked through his own dark valley. The children were living with an emotionally and spiritually absent father and with a mother who was "worn to a frazzle" and struggling with menopause. The winds of the trials were blowing fiercely and were threatening to destroy my entire family – God had His work cut out for Him as we struggled to stay together.

# CHAPTER VII

# WINDS OF SICKNESS, DEPRESSION & SPIRITUAL ABUSE

After Jean's death there came waves of sicknesses and depression that threatened to engulf my family. Louis was already struggling with a Thyroid condition and then got diagnosed with Diabetes. When we were doing ministry after Jean's death, a great betrayal began the down-slide of Louis' trust in Christians and his walk with the Lord. In a different chapter, I will speak to you, the reader, about spiritual abuse, control, and betrayal from Christians and Pastors. Right now, I intend to just share about how different events from various churches we attended caused great difficulty in our ministry. Louis and I went to many different churches as we rose up ministries in worship dance, children's church, Missionettes and Royal Rangers, teaching about the Feasts of the Lord, and so forth. When one travels over twenty years' time doing this kind of ministry, one finds oneself in many different situations. During these times of betrayal and abuse, Louis became disillusioned and disengaged. I, on the other hand, continued to press into the Lord and continued forward in ministry even to my own detriment.

When Louis became disillusioned with church people, his walk with the Lord became a roller coaster ride. He would be on his ups and then would plummet down. Louis tended to be obsessive / compulsive in many areas of his life. He smoked and was consumed with TV and screens. Now this does not seem to be so "out of the ordinary" for one, but in our life it was detrimental. The television and computer consumed all his time at home. He was physically present in the house, but was emotionally, spiritually, and mentally "checked out." He would go months where he would watch television and play computer games from the moment he walked in the door until late into the evenings (11 – 12 midnight). Don't get me wrong, he was a good provider as far as going to work and bringing home a paycheck, but as far as giving into the family, he did not do this. The first seven years of our marriage, he was a wonderful father and husband. Then Jean died and the church betrayal happened and after that it was all downhill. I can remember a few months after Jean's funeral; I got angry with Louis and yelled at him: "For goodness sake, God did not fall off the throne just because the church hurt us!!!!" I was so angry because I was fast losing the wonderful, godly man I had married. He started to refuse to be any part of the children's lives. He complained whenever he would have to go to recitals, sports events, church events, in fact, any event that had to do with the children or us as a family. He would start fights purposefully so that I would finally get angry and tell him to stay home and I would take the kids myself. He knew this would work, so he would push until I blew, and then he would get to stay home. This type of behavior went on until a few months before he passed away. Life became one argument after another, day in and day out. To add "fuel to the fire" as they say, his health continued to get worse. When they diagnosed him with Diabetes his sugars were in the 700's. Normal sugar levels are in the low 100's for a healthy person. His A1C was fourteen, and normal was seven. The doctors were astounded that he was even walking around; he should have been in a coma. Well, what we found out later was that he probably had Leukemia in his body at the time of the Diabetes diagnosis and we did not even know. The Leukemia would make it near impossible for his body to regulate his sugars. While the doctors tried to regulate his sugars, they remained at an unstable high. They would never get below the 150's. After a while, Louis did not care anymore, and he began to eat large amounts of ice cream, chocolate bars, and so forth before he would go to bed. His sugars would go out of control and the cycle would go round and round. I once told him that I was so tired of spinning around and around on the same "hamster wheel". Dementia like symptoms occur when one's sugar levels go out of control. We spent the next ten years with Louis behaving irrationally and many times violent because he could not seem to control his behavior. He would forget all sorts of things (like his children's names, birthdays, how to go to the store, and so forth). He was unstable, to say the least. I can remember begging him to go to the doctor and find out what was going on with his mind only to get into a screaming argument and being accused of "nagging" and "controlling" him. All this went hand in hand with the fact that I became highly allergic to nicotine. We lived in a rented house, after selling our home of 20 years, and there was black mold. This mold got into my lungs and body and caused me to nearly die. Because of this I developed Asthma and allergies to many different things, inclusive of nicotine. As a result, anytime we would be intimate (i.e. kissing, intercourse), I would end up extremely sick and in the hospital. It got to where even if I touched someone who smoked I would break out in the hives and start having breathing issues. If we would be intimate, my bladder would bleed and shut down for days. The doctor finally told Louis that if he did not quit smoking, he would ultimately kill me. The amount of medicine I had to take to get better was destroying my kidney and liver. Louis tried so hard to quit but failed miserably time and time again. When he could not successfully quit, he started to lie and secretly take money from the bank account causing it to overdraft numerous times in a month. We did not have very much money because we had eight children, so this would result in huge fights. During these fights, Louis would lose control and call me horrible names, throw and break things, and eventually resulted in him physically hurting me. During the fights, I would yell and cry telling him he was an awful husband and father. Sadly enough, the children witnessed and overheard these fights. The constant tension and strain of the broken marriage began to have grave effects upon our children. There were many times I would plan on leaving Louis and would actually go as far as finding a place to go. Then, God would whoosh in and somehow speak to me to stay and try and work things out and fix things. I would finally relent, stay, and the "hamster wheel" would spin again. When I look back, I often wonder if I made a mistake by staying, but I felt God wanted me to stay and persevere. Thankfully, the Bible says, "And we know that God causes all things to work together for good to those who love God, to those who are called according to His purpose" (Romans 8:28). So, whether I made a bad choice or not, I knew that my God would be faithful to work it all out for our good. An event that stemmed from a miracle is something I will share with you, the reader, so you can grasp how much God desires for us to keep our marriage commitment even when there is complete chaos. He is bigger than the chaos. In October, 2010 we were approaching our twenty- year anniversary. Life was spinning out of control even then. I went to a couple of the church leaders and explained to them that Louis' abuse had brought me to the place that I could not live with him anymore. I did not want to continue with the smoking trial that kept me in constant sickness or celibacy (one or the other), and I could not imagine another day of fighting. So I told them that I wanted to separate from Louis until God could deliver him. I packed his bags and we met with Louis to tell him that he would have to find somewhere else to live. Louis told me that he was shocked, and so scared to leave us. He ended up living with friends and then with our son, John Jr. By Thanksgiving, Louis had been gone a few weeks. We were in contact with one another, and I told him I did not want a divorce, but that he needed to be freed from addiction and anger. On Thanksgiving morning we were having dinner with my extended family at my house. I was praying early in the morning about what to do with my marriage. A strong wind gushed over me (now mind you, all the windows were closed because it was very cold outside), and the Lord spoke quietly in the wind to me. He stated that I was to take forty days and speak scripture into Louis and pray for him. Then God said the strangest thing, He used Moses and the forty years in the wilderness to encourage me that it could be done. He also used Jesus and His forty days in the dessert being tried by the devil to tell me that I could pass this test. God went even further though and told me that I had to renew my wedding vows to Louis on our 20th anniversary. I could not even imagine this. I told God that I did not understand. Our marriage was dangling by a thread, yet I was to recommit to this man and continue in our traumatic life. I thought for sure I was hearing voices. At this point I did a "Gideon." What is that you ask? In the Bible Gideon had to do something that seemed impossible so he threw up a "fleece" to God. Here is the story:

> *AFTER the death of Joshua, the Israelites turned away from God, and served idols. Therefore the evils came upon them of which the bad been warned by Moses and Joshua. But at different times God, seeing their distress, raised up "judges" to deliver them from their enemies, and to judge over them. The first of these judges was named Othniel. He was Caleb's nephew. The last was Samuel. One that lived about one hundred years before Samuel was named Gideon.*
>
> *The Israelites at this time were in great trouble. They were hiding in dens and caves because of the Midianites, who had conquered them and overrun their country. When their corn was ripe these enemies came and destroyed it, so altogether they were in a sad plight.*
>
> *One day Gideon was threshing wheat in a secluded place, so as to escape the notice of the Midianites, when an angel from God appeared to him, bidding him to go and save the Israelites from their foes. Gideon obeyed the command: but before commencing the battle he much desired a sign from God showing that He would give the Israelites the victory. The sign Gideon asked for was, that when he laid a fleece of wool on the ground, if the victory were to be his, then the fleece should be wet and the ground dry.*
>
> *He placed the Wool on the ground, and taking it up the next morning found it wet, although the ground was dry. So he knew God had answered him as he desired. But he was not quite satisfied He begged God for a second sign.*
> *This time the ground was to be wet and the fleece of wool*

> *dry. God gave him this sign also: and then Gideon felt sure that the Israelites would be victorious over the Midianites.*
> (Favorite Bible Stories in Simple English - Gideon and the Fleece. Edited and Adapted From Antique Book in His Library © By James Dearmore, July, 1999)

I was desperately trying to decipher this word from the Lord, so I threw up, what I thought, was an impossible fleece. I told God that if this truly was Him, I would need someone to come up and give me a wedding dress without knowing anything about the renewal ceremony, and then I requested a bright, pink object (even if it was a stick of gum) to be given to me. Now, what is the chance of both of these happening? I even told God that I needed it to be done by December 31st because our 20th anniversary was January 5th, and I would need a week to plan a wedding. Sure enough, God met the demands. As Christians sometimes say, God always seems to wait until the "midnight hour" though. That is exactly what He did! It was December 31st, and Louis and I were scheduled to go for a date night. The first amazing thing that happened was Louis told me that he wished he had a ring. I took off the ring on my left hand and handed it to him. I had no idea what he was going to do; then he asked me to remarry him on our 20th wedding anniversary. He had no idea that God had already told me that we needed to do this. I let him know that God had instructed me to renew my vows with him but that I needed God to do two different things for me. He asked me if I would tell him what they were, but I refused because I did not want to chance anyone being able to say that they overheard us, and so they approached me. As a side note: earlier that week the Lord had told me to go and buy new wedding rings. I even saw a vision of the ring I was to buy. It was a three strand ring with pink and black stones wrapped by a diamond band. We did not have any money. Funny enough, my wedding ring had shattered into four pieces (for no apparent reason) a few weeks earlier. To me, that was a prophetic sign of our marriage as far as I was concerned. I told the Lord I did not have the money to buy new rings. He assured me He would pay for them. Back to the date: we were at Ruby Tuesdays' restaurant and a lady that we had known from years before asked us what we were doing there. We explained that we were on a date. She did not seem to think much about that, but a few minutes later she came to our table and told me that she had a wedding dress for me so that I could renew my wedding vows. I was speechless. God had met my first demand. Out of the blue, a woman came and gave me a dress without knowing anything (remember, this was my first fleece unto God). God whispered in my ear that He had met my first demand. It was 8:00 p.m. on December 31st when that happened. I broke down and told Louis that what this lady had done was my first fleece and God had just met it. He asked me the second one, but I still would not tell him. By the way, the wedding dress was the exact size I needed. When the date was finished, we went home; it was 10:36 p.m. when one of my daughters walked upstairs and said, "Mom, I was going to throw this out, but God told me to come up and give it to you." You guessed it, she handed me a bright pink ticket to a store. I could not believe it, God had met my second fleece (someone would come up and give me a bright pink object and tell me that God told them to give it to me). God whispered in my ear that He had met my second fleece by midnight on December 31st. How could I argue with God? I told Louis about the second fleece and how God met it, so we started planning a wedding.

    The next day was January 1st, and the Lord told me that Louis and I needed to go and get the rings. I did not even think the stores were open, but they were. We went to the mall and at exactly one minute to closing God directed us to go into a jewelry store. We stepped in, and I found the exact ring laying in the case. I could not believe my eyes. The exact ring in my vision was laying right there, and it was 40% clearance. Louis looked and found his ring also. The problem was, together they were $4200.00. There was no way we could swing that kind of money (even on a credit card). The lady waiting on us kept telling us that we were the cutest couple she ever saw. She finally said, "Wait here, I will be right back." When she returned, she offered us both rings at $1000.00 with a life time warranty. I was completely flabbergasted. We accepted the deal and left. By the end of the week, the Lord was faithful to do exactly what He said he would do. A check for the exact amount of the rings came in the mail. Amazing – the Lord had done exactly as He said He would do.

To top everything off, we ended up getting a church for free, donated food, new dresses for the girls to wear, and everything for the wedding, and all of it cost only $150.00. There were thirty plus people, and it was an absolutely stunning day. God had His will done, and Louis moved back home.

Even though the renewals of vows were completed, life was definitely not a "bed of roses." We still had child issues because of bad choices made by them, and Louis continued to struggle with a complete deliverance.  The amazing thing to me was that God used me to help many people get delivered and free from strongholds and demons, but my own husband did not trust me and would not allow me to help him.  And then we met "The Prophet."

   One Saturday I had come to a breaking point.  Louis and I had gotten into a terrible argument, again.  He did not come to church another Saturday.  I was crying out to God on the way to the church and telling Him that I needed a prophet to come into my life to deliver my husband, a prophet.  I was so angry, that I told God that I wanted "Moses!"  I did not care how he came, but I wanted Moses.  When I got to church, I was standing on stage and playing tambourines when in walked a man who was wearing robes, carrying a staff, had hair to his shoulders, and had a beard.  I was so stunned that I even stopped playing tambourines.  I looked to heaven and said, "You sent me Moses! You actually sent Moses?"  I heard God chuckle and say, "You asked for a prophet like Moses, so here he is."  After service God gave me a vision of this man's feet on fire and gave me a prophetic word that He wanted me to speak to this man.  You must understand, I had not prophesied in a very long time.  So after church, he walked up to the altar for prayer.  I thought

I would be clever, and so I stood very far behind him and just whispered the word that God had given me. I called it "prophesying into the air." I felt that I had done the job sufficiently. God reprimanded me and told me that I needed to deliver it directly to him, so when he went downstairs for fellowship, I followed. I approached this man and told him I had a word from the Lord for him. When I gave it, he shouted out praises unto God and told me that I was very accurate. He then called me a prophetess and gave me a direct word from God. A situation had happened with our daughter, Michaela, earlier that week. She had actually run away from home. He told me the exact thing that had happened in my home and then told me that she would be returning home to us. He said, "Because you, a prophetess, were faithful to give a word to a prophet, God will answer your prayers for your daughter and she will return." I sobbed so hard because I had been asking that all along. His word came to pass, she did return home, and God completely restored her back to us. As time went on, the prophet became our dear friend, and God faithfully used him to help Louis get delivered of many strongholds and ultimately, helped him to die well.  Louis was not the only one who was struggling with various strongholds; I had my own issues arise.

All the while we were walking through these different phases of trials; I was struggling through intense Menopause.  It hit hard!!!!  Hot flashes, mood swings, migraines, out of control menstrual cycles, and periods of depression.  Louis and I went many months at a time not being intimate. No kissing, hugging, no touching, no sexual intercourse, NOTHING!  This strained our marriage even more – life was crumbling.  I would find myself crying for no apparent reason and thoughts of ending the miserable existence would flood through my brain.  My fuse was short, and life was tough.  I began to crawl inside a shell of my own and ceased to want friends, relationships, or church life.  I still trudged to church week after week with the kids, only to find myself further and further from people.  I knew one thing though; I loved Jesus more than ever now.  I never found myself angry with God – often confused, but not angry.  The harder the Devil pushed and squeezed on my life and marriage, the more determined I became to make it work.  I hated the Devil with a vehement hatred I did not even know could exist.  The thing that amazed me was how God continued to use my husband and me, even when our life was shattering before our very eyes. After I wrote the first book, *Thou He Slay Me, Yet Shall I Praise Him,* I found that God opened up an enormous deliverance ministry in my life. God had prophesied that the book would bring much healing and deliverance to individuals and families. Right after I got the book in print, I was asked to go to a conference of a lady pastor who did deliverance ministry. The night before the conference, all hell broke loose in my house. At midnight I told the Lord I was not going because it was too difficult. I fell asleep and I had a dream. I saw a pastor (whom I had never seen before) walk out onto a platform and start preaching about deliverance ministry. The Lord woke me early in the morning and told me to go to the conference. I left and arrived about 8:00 a.m. I was greeted by the lady who invited me (who incidentally had been one of the proof readers of the book) and watched as the exact same pastor that was in my dream showed up on the platform. I was shocked and amazed. She started by saying that God had woken her at 5:00 a.m. and told her that a lady would be at the conference and she was to depart deliverance ministry into this woman. She said that she did not know exactly who that person was, but that God would reveal it to her as the day went on. When she said this, the Lord spoke to me and told me that I was the woman. I was taken aback by the Lord. I knew I had been in many types of ministry, including prophetic ministry, up to this point but did not know much about doing deliverances. God had spent many years declaring to me and to the church (through many people) that I was a prophetess. I resisted that for many years because, I don't know about you, but the prophets during the Bible times never had it easy. I did not want to be one of them. Finally, I relented and accepted that I was a prophetess and would need to minister how God used me as a prophetess. To continue - at lunch the lady that asked me to the conference led me over and introduced me to the pastor. When our hands touched in a handshake an anointing that felt like an electric shock hit our hands. The woman looked into my eyes and stated, "You are the lady God told me about this morning! I need to pray over you at the end of service and impart deliverance ministry upon you." She mentioned the book I wrote, and told me that God would greatly use me to heal and deliver many people. At the end of service, there was a very long line of people for prayer. I had to get home, but I waited as long as I possibly could. I was on the opposite side of the auditorium as the pastor. She had spent about an hour doing deliverance ministry, and I waited. Finally, she was sitting slumped in a chair, utterly exhausted from ministering, and I got up to leave. I told God, I could not wait anymore. I stood up to leave, and I saw her bolt up out of her chair and turn and spot me. She motioned for me to come over to her, and so I did. She laid hands on me and imparted deliverance. When she did this, she told me that I would start to get phone calls and people would ask me to come over and pray for them to be delivered, cleansed, and healed. I thanked her and left. Little did I know, the next morning the phone would start ringing and would continue on for twelve years. I found myself going home to home, place to place, while a little prayer intercession group beseeched God on my behalf. God would strategically put me in places where I could learn different types of deliverance ministry and then would send me out to do the very thing I had learned. I ended up praying for many different types of individuals; they ranged from Christians who had demonic happenings in their life, to believers and unbelievers who were demon indwelled or tormented. I prayed deliverance for witches, voodoo dabblers, wiccans, a lady with cannibal ancestors, multiple personality disorders which was a result from severe sexual abuse, satanically ritually abused individuals, individuals with homes full of poltergeist, Satan worshipers, and so forth. Every kind of demon, witch, and other dark spirit seemed to come into my path. Strange things would be placed in my path and God would have me pray. While this went on, hell was breaking loose in my home. As others were set free, my family seemed to be pounded on harder and harder. Once I told my sister that I felt like on hell's walls was written, "For a good time, go attack Lily's life". This seems humorous now, but back then it seemed very real. I wanted to quit so very often, and God would encourage me to keep going while promising to take care of my family and life. Good thing that God can use any kind of vessel, because I felt very inadequate and weak. People would tell me I was amazing and the strongest woman they had ever met. Inside I would be telling the Lord that I felt very tired and worn out. I would think, "If they only knew what was going on within my own family, they would be judging me harshly." The Lord remains faithful and is a grace-filled God. In 1 Corinthian 1:27 it states, "But God chose the foolish things of the world to shame the wise; God chose the weak things of the world to shame the strong." That is exactly what He was doing, using my weakness to show His strength, and the foolish chaos of my life, to show His wisdom.

If there was a doubt in my mind that I was to be in this deliverance ministry, God used an Occult member to put to rest my doubts. About a year or two into deliverance ministry, I was in the parking lot of the church, and it was late evening. Even though it was cold and drizzly, I was talking with another woman ministering to her. My children were all in the van waiting, and the parking lot was empty. Suddenly, a car dropped a man off at the end of the parking lot. He started walking toward us and was obviously part of an occult group. He had occult signs tattooed all over; he had a skin-head, and was very scary. I looked at the woman and stated, "Either we are going to die today, be raped, or God has something in mind here!" The lady was so scared. I could not even tell the emotions that were going through me, but I started to pray inside. The man approached us and looked at me and told me that he was running from "them" because "they" were trying to kill him. I asked him, "Who are them?" He replied, "The demons." He said that he used to go to this church that we were standing by when he was a young boy. He stated that a man had picked him up, and when they were passing by, he heard a voice say, (which he claimed was the voice of God) stop here and get out. He said the same voice told him that the lady (which he stated was me) standing in the parking lot could help him. To shorten a long story, I ended up praying with this man and gave him a warm blanket. He wanted me to take him to a "safe place" so, I decided that "Union Gospel Mission" was a good place, and I knew the minster there could help him. In my heart, I knew that I could not let him get in my van with me and my children, so I asked God for some help because I did not know what to do. Immediately, a very large man in a truck came from behind the church and drove up and looked at me. He said, "Did you need my help, I'm here to help you?" I was stunned. Sure that God had sent an angel, I asked the man to take this gentleman to the Mission and ask the minister to help him. I concluded that if God would tell a member of the Occult that I could help get him free, then I must be on the right track. Through these twelve years, I cannot begin to express how many souls were delivered from torment and bondage. When I look back, I can say that it was all worth the "beatings" my family took from the enemy. The testimonies poured in from the book and the prayer times. God be praised and glorified, because I couldn't have done it without Him.

My own health was compromised through the stress and strain of those years of trials. I ended up with Fibromyalgia, and I still get migraines each month; the mood swings have calmed down, and the joy of my salvation has been restored. I see life as a gift given every day. During this time, one of my daughters got Fibromyalgia. This condition keeps her in constant pain. Another one of my daughters got a medical condition, due to her life choices, that will be with her the rest of her life (if the Lord chooses not to heal her), and it will be a trial she will have to face, my son has emotional difficulties dealing with all the trauma of life, and another of my daughters had to spend six months in a recovery center for depression, cutting, and other issues. All in all though, the bumps and bruises have come and gone; God has continued to work and is continuing to work on the healing and salvation of my children and me. There is still much emotional hurt and mistrust that God needs to repair, but He will prove faithful to do that also.

During the times that the storm raged, I had stated that God continued to have me stay. Shortly before Louis got diagnosed with

Leukemia, I got weary of the battle and had finally decided I was going. My last straw was when we had a fight, and he told me I was purely evil and had called me a wicked b#@%^. I cried so hard, I did not think anymore tears could come. Over the years I had watched him break things, rage uncontrollably, jump out of our moving vehicle at thirty miles per hour because he was so angry, bust up his computer, destroy entire walls of pictures, lock me in rooms and back me against walls only to find him spitting on me and raging nasty words at me. He would tell me he never did these things because he could not remember them. This was so frustrating because it seemed to be true. The uncontrollable sugars were causing his memory to fail, and I was convinced he had become Bi-Polar. I finally broke and told Louis that I was physically in the house, but had left in every other possible way, mentally, emotionally, and spiritually. I told him our marriage was over, and I had regretted the day I had married him. I told him I could not take any more emotional, physical, or verbal abuse. He did not seem to care; he had given up on us and had crawled inside himself to the point where he showed no emotion or remorse for anything he was doing. The next day, I got busy finding me and the children a place to go; I was getting DIVORCED. I knew God had told me not to, but my longsuffering was over. I told God, "I know you want me to stay, but this man is destroying me in every way possible. I am not perfect like you, and I cannot endure anymore." My mind was set – I was leaving! As a side note, during really traumatic times in our lives God would always warn us when things were going to be extremely difficult. He warned us before Jean was going to die, when our fifteen year old daughter was pregnant because of a "professing 'Christian'" counselor molesting her, and so forth. When I gave up completely, an amazing thing happened, God came flooding in. I knew God's instruction was for me to stay, so I told Him I was completely finished, and the only way I would stay is if an angel with a flaming sword came into my room. That night, a ten-foot (or bigger) angel walked in my room and in his hand was a flaming sword. He told me that I had to stay, but that there was going to be a trial bigger than I had ever experienced and that I would need to be strengthened. He told me to take his hand and come with him to the top of the mountain. I was so weak; I could not even lift my hand to grab his. He grasped my hand, and we went together to the top of that mountain. There sat Jesus. He poured into me strength and love. He shared with me that He was always with me and my family and would be with us when the hottest trial of all hit. This was in December, 2012. I found my spirit back inside my body with a new strength to move forward in my ordained race.

During all these trials, the Lord had instructed me to go to college. I thought He had lost His marbles (does God have marbles? ☺). God started speaking to my heart for many months about going to college. Finally, after a year of this tugging at my heart, I enrolled in a local Christian University. I graduated in December, 2014, YEAH!!!! Five long years it took me. I got my degree in Health Psychology – isn't that funny? Me a counselor – after all the trauma of my own life. God told me that He wanted me to be a Bereavement Counselor. During those five years of college, all these trials were going on. What I found interesting, every class I had to take seemed to correlate with the trial in our life at the time. When I had to take "Grief and Loss" my husband's three brothers, two sisters, and my ex-husband all died in the course of three years. When I had to take "Trauma and Crises" our youngest daughter had to go into a recovery center and then got pregnant when her professing Christian counselor molested her, our third daughter ran away from home (only to find herself in poverty and a promiscuous life) Louis got Leukemia. I had to work sixty to seventy hours a week to pay tuition for the recovery center, go to college thirty hours per week, be mom and be a wife who was taking care of a sick husband. I found myself, counseling ME through the course of nine months' time. God also used my professors to speak life, peace, strength, and comfort into my soul. The Bible declares that we are the hands and feet of Christ. I found this to be so true during these five years. My professors became God's mouth piece, His hands, and His feet. It was a blessed time in my life even though it was overwhelming.

February 2013 arrived and it was time for me to enroll in spring classes. I knew that the hottest trial ever loomed on the horizon. Life was a little bit calmer right now. Our daughter was out of the recovery center and doing pretty good, Louis was feeling better and had a new job making more money, and our other daughter had come home after running away and was better. I could not see why I needed to finish college, so I told God I was going to quit. He spoke sternly to me and told me that I needed to finish my degree. I only had a little over a year and a half left. I told God, I was tired, worn out, exhausted in every way possible, and wanted to be done. I told Him that we were financially okay, and I did not need this degree because my income was a second income. Finally, God said the strangest thing to me. He said, "Lily, you will need your degree because Louis will not be here to support you." This was the second week of February. I was dumb-founded. What did the Lord mean? I asked Him, "What do you mean, where is he going?" Remember, God had just sent an angel two months earlier to tell me to stay. I was baffled. Finally God said to me, "Louis is going to die, I am taking him home to me." That made things clearer to me. I signed up for class. The following week, Louis was diagnosed with a rare form of Leukemia, Chronic Lymphocytic Leukemia – Deletion 17. This meant that he did not have Chromosome 17 so the Leukemia was fast growing.

Life at home was better, but not great. God had done much healing and deliverance in our home, but there was a lot left. Our youngest daughter was still struggling with anger, depression, and other emotions – the other children were feeling the strain of the years of unhappiness and stress. Now we all had to find strength to walk through the hottest trial ever – death and child- molestation! Oh how I found myself leaning heavily into the Lord, as I felt alone, angry, sad, frustrated, and extremely exhausted. But there was even more grace and mercy for the coming time! Even now as I look back, the words of this song that my daughter, Michaela, once sang to me resonate truer than ever.

**"Oceans (Where Feet May Fail)"**

*You call me out upon the waters*
*The great unknown where feet may fail*
*And there I find You in the mystery*
*In oceans deep*
*My faith will stand*

*And I will call upon Your name*
*And keep my eyes above the waves*
*When oceans rise*
*My soul will rest in Your embrace*
*For I am Yours and You are mine*

*Your grace abounds in deepest waters*
*Your sovereign hand*
*Will be my guide*
*Where feet may fail and fear surrounds me*
*You've never failed and You won't start now*

*So I will call upon Your name*
*And keep my eyes above the waves*
*When oceans rise*
*My soul will rest in Your embrace*
*For I am Yours and You are mine*

*Spirit lead me where my trust is without borders*

*Let me walk upon the waters*
*Wherever You would call me*
*Take me deeper than my feet could ever wander*
*And my faith will be made stronger*
*In the presence of my Savior*

*Oh, Jesus, you're my God!*

*I will call upon your name*
*Keep my eyes above the waves*
*My soul will rest in Your embrace*
*I am Yours and You are mine*     (*HILLSONG UNITED LYRIC)


2 Corinthians 9:8 states this, "And God *is* able to make all grace abound toward you, that you, always having all sufficiency in all *things,* may have abundance for every good work." Lamentations 3:22-23 states this, "The steadfast love of the LORD never ceases; *his mercies* never come to an end; they *are new every morning*; great is your faithfulness." God proved faithful in two promises over the next year and a half of my family's life.

# CHAPTER VIII

# STORMS OF LEUKEMIA & DEATH

Fire burns hot, just as trials burn hot, and ironically "fire" was what brought the news of Louis' Leukemia diagnosis. It was February 2013, and a fire broke out at Louis' work place. He was the Environmental Service Director (oversaw maintenance department, housekeeping, and the grounds), so when the fire broke out he had to stay and help evacuate the Assisted Living. This took twelve hours, and he was exposed to a lot of smoke. The next day he was very sick with a cough. His boss told him he had to go to the doctor and be checked out for smoke inhalation. When they drew his blood, his white count was at approximately 100,000. That is well over ten times what it should be. The next day the doctor told him that he had Leukemia, and that he needed to go and see an oncologist immediately. After seeing the oncologist, he was tested for the kind of Leukemia he had. He ended up having Chronic Lymphocytic Leukemia – deletion 17. This meant that he did not have Chromosome 17 in his body and that the cancer would be fast growing. Louis pressed into God to see what His plan was, and I found myself on my own journey to figure out how I was to help Louis and the kids during this sad and difficult time.

The first thing Louis did was to search the Word of God to find a scripture that would help him understand God's plan for his life. Within the week, Louis came to me and told me that he believed God had shared with him Psalm 84. He stated that this was the Psalm that would set the course of the next however many months or years of his life. As we sifted through this scripture the particular part that stood out was verses 5-7: "Blessed is the man whose strength is in You, whose heart is set on pilgrimage. As they pass through the Valley of Baca, they make it a spring; the rain also covers it with pools. They go from strength to strength; each one appears before God in Zion." When Louis brought this passage to me, he told me he believed I would be able to help him determine what it meant. So we decided to go into the Bible and do a study on some of the words. We started with the word, Baca. This literally meant thorns and thistles – so we concluded that the Leukemia and pain that would go along with it would be the thorns and thistles.

Baca also inferred sorrow and sadness. We understood that preparing for death would definitely include sorrow and sadness. The next part of the verse talks of making the valley a spring; this became an understanding that even though we were to walk this very sad and hard walk, we were to walk it in a way that would prove to be a testimony to others along with our own family. At the same time, Louis got the scripture verse Romans 14:8 which states, "If we live, we live for the Lord; and if we die, we die for the Lord. So, whether we live or die, we belong to the Lord." When he quoted this verse to me, he made a bold statement. Louis told me that he was going to believe God for healing, but if God decided not to heal him and he had to die, he would glorify God either way. He literally told me that "if I die, I will die unto the Lord, and if I live, I will live unto the Lord. Either way, I want my life to glorify the Lord." So this was the decision, we would pray for healing, but if God decided he was going to take Louis home, we would still rejoice. There was a dear brother in the Lord who decided he would have a faith walk with Louis, and so every evening he came over and prayed with Louis. In addition, Louis believed he was not to take any treatment. When we sat with the Oncologist, we were told because of the type of Leukemia, the success rate for Chemotherapy helping was very low. They offered to let him go to Texas to do experimental treatment (Louis called it a "lab rat" effort), but he turned them down – not wanting to feel sick from a bunch of experimental drugs. Prayer was the only avenue of cure that we were faced with. The weeks turned into months, and our marriage relationship really didn't change much, but the arguing stopped. I had told Louis that I was there to help him die well, and that commitment would stand. So, even though the circumstances surrounding our marriage and life were still very strained, I stayed and loved him through this difficult walk. Problem number two presented itself though - our 15 year old daughter came home pregnant. Around the time that Louis was diagnosed with Leukemia, she went into a very severe depression which we could not really understand. After finding out the circumstances of how she became pregnant, the revelation of what was happening brought light to why she was depressed. I will share this story in the next chapter, but for now, what is important to point out, is that as a family we were to face circumstances that would forever change the course of our family unit and how it functioned. I found myself having to lean upon God in a way that I never even thought was possible. God would ask things of me as a wife, mother, and church member that I really did not think I could do – but as the Word of God states in 2 Corinthians 12:9-10, "And He has said to me, 'My grace is sufficient for you, for power is perfected in weakness.' Most gladly, therefore, I will rather boast about my weaknesses, so that the power of Christ may dwell in me. Therefore I am well content with weaknesses, with insults, with distresses, with persecutions, with difficulties, for Christ's sake; for when I am weak, then I am strong."

Eleven months had passed since Louis' diagnosis, and I found myself worn out emotionally, physically, spiritually, and mentally. I was still working forty plus hours per week, going to college with double-load classes, helping care for a sick and dying husband, and helping care for an angry, resentful, pregnant, and irrational fifteen-year old daughter. All the while, I found that I had no support from anyone who could understand. I tried a few counselors, but only to have them tell me that they did not know where to start in my life because there were so many trials and they did not know how to begin to help me. I found that God and my school courses were the only places I could turn for help. Each school course I took ended up lining up with the very things going on in my life. I was actually living out each Psychology course and found that the information on how to counsel others in trouble became a very helpful avenue for my own life situations. One very difficult thing I found myself dealing with and felt that I had nowhere to turn, nor did I exactly understand what to do or say, was the "faith-healing" movement of believers that were bombarding Louis and my life. These believers were the ones who believed that when one became sick, the only way was God's healing. They preached that God would not allow a Christian to be sick or die, and if that individual died they would be in sin because of his or her lack of faith. Even our own adopted daughter would tell us "faith-healing" things like this. She even inferred that if her father died, he would die in a state of sin and would not go to heaven. I was flabbergasted! I did not understand any of this – because, of course, in the past many of our friends and relatives who were Christians had gotten sick and died. There were even ridiculous words come over Louis like "you have had spiritual radiation and the Leukemia is gone!" (Only to find out at the next Oncology visit that it had gotten worse). This type of behavior and words only proved to bring false hope and confusion. After about eight months of believing God to heal Louis, I felt the Lord prompt me to stop praying for healing and change my prayers to encompass the children and me.  I started to pray for strength to walk through death, peace and comfort to walk through sorrow, and boldness to stand firm on what God had revealed to Louis and I about his death.  I was accused of killing my husband because I did not "pray hard enough" or did not "speak enough scripture and life" over him.  This type of behavior proved to only push me further from the church.  I already did not trust Pastors or church members because of all the weirdness of what we dealt with over the years, but now couple it with a pregnant daughter from a professing Christian counselor/minister molesting her and a bunch of crazy "faith healing" people and this was recipe for disaster.  Finally, March 10, 2014, Louis had to quit work.  His boss had been wonderful up to this point and had revamped his work so that as the Leukemia and fatigue got worse he could continue to work.  It finally became evident to his boss that he could not perform his duties anymore.  Louis could not even walk from his office to the lobby at work without having to stop and rest due to his weakness.  His chest, arms, legs, hands, and feet were continually burning.   Louis was called into his boss' office and was given the news that he could not continue at work. This devastated him because it was what he called "my death sentence." Louis stated that he felt he was destined to just wait at home for death. February and March proved to be a time that Louis had made a decision that he would get blood transfusions so that he could feel better. His Hemoglobin level had plummeted dangerously low, and he could barely stand up without wanting to pass out. The blood transfusions were not a cure, but a way to feel a little better. He could not go on Hospice while receiving these. I felt that they were a small bandage put upon a gaping wound, but I had promised Louis that whatever he decided in his Cancer walk, I would support those decisions. These transfusions were about $7500.00 apiece. He was receiving two of them per week. During the last two years, we had already spent approximately $30,000.00 on medical care for Louis' other health issues, so this was a large amount of money. To shorten a very lengthy money discussion, we had to come up with another $15,000.00 in insurance deductible to continue the transfusions past April first. If the transfusions stopped, it would be just a couple weeks and Louis would be dead. The transfusions were the only things keeping his red blood cell count high enough so that his blood could sustain the oxygen level he needed.

On the morning of March 28th, Louis and I had a discussion on how we did not have the money to continue the transfusions, and they would have to stop. We made the decision that he would go on hospice to prepare to die. I had so much guilt! I felt I had placed a price ($15,000.00) on his life and there was no other option. I fell asleep crying and praying that night. As I have testified throughout this entire book, God is a good and faithful God. Louis' final transfusion was to be on March 29th and then hospice would start on March 31st. Again, I was plagued with guilt because of lack of money to continue the transfusions. Even though they weren't a cure, they would help prolong his life a bit longer. Then an astounding event happened. The morning of March 29th the Oncology nurse called and told me that Louis could no longer receive any more transfusions. I was confused, so I asked her to explain. She stated that Louis' own blood had built up antibodies that were detecting the new blood as a germ. These antibodies were "eating" the new blood, and so it was useless to give him anymore transfusions. The transfusions were actually causing the Leukemia to progress even faster. I could not believe my ears; the very thing that we decided had to be stopped anyway. I started to cry and explain to her the situation; she was very compassionate and said, "It seems God has provided a way of guilt-relief for you." When I shared the news with Louis, he simply stated, "Well, it seems the decision is made by God." I will get ready to go home to the Lord. The following day, we contacted hospice and it was set to start on March 31st.

Louis started seeking God about what was to come for his life (no matter what length of time he was given). The Lord took him into Genesis 47 and shared with him about Jacob and his seventeen years in Egypt. Louis stated that God had explained to him in this scripture that Jacob spent those seventeen years building a nation, and then requested that his body be taken out of Egypt when he died and buried in the promise land with his ancestors. Then Louis told me that God had spoken clearly to his heart and told him that he would live for seventeen days and die on April 18th at which time he would be taken up to heaven (the promised land). Louis was also given very clear instruction on what he was to do those seventeen days. For the next seventeen days, he obeyed the Lord and did all

God asked. He spent his days making sure he had forgiven all those in life who had hurt him, settled any issues between him and others, preached the gospel to his only unsaved brother (who gave his life to the Lord), and finally ended up leading two teenagers to the Lord that week - then came the morning of April 18th.

The dream was in progress – 3:00 a.m. was the time on the clock when I awoke out of this dream. I was lying on an eagle and soaring through the air. There were multiple storms in progress (hail, snow blizzard, rainstorm, tsunami, and so forth). The eagle was soaring through the storms with me on its back, and I was not being affected by these storms. I then heard the Lord say to me, "Lily, it has begun. Wake up; it is time! Louis is coming home to me!" At that very moment, Louis yelled for me. He could not breathe anymore and was suffocating. I went out into my living room to experience the most amazing transition from this life into eternal life. Upon arriving into my living room, Louis' first response was to ask me to overdose him because the pain was so great. I told Louis I would not do that because I could not live with that decision. He was very desperate, so he then told me that Jesus needed to come and get him. I said, "Okay then, let's ask Jesus to come and get you." The Lord then spoke to my heart and told me to open the Bible. I flipped it open to Psalm 34; "The Lord inclines His ear to the righteous man and delivers him from his anguish." I stated, "There it is, He is ready to take you out of this anguish." I grabbed Louis' hand, and we prayed that Jesus would come and get him. Within about thirty seconds, Louis breathed his last breath. The most amazing thing was what happened to his physical body. He had been in anguish and was unable to breath. Because of this, he was curled into a ball and was pulling at his clothing and chest because of the inability to get enough oxygen and the pain in his body. So when he passed away, he had been in a fetal position with his hand clutching the bed railing. As soon as he breathed his last breath, he was laid out in a relaxed position with his ankles crossed and his hands gently lay on his stomach. His face was turned to the window looking up toward the sun. I was not in a position where I was able to see this happen, so I do not know if an angel came and placed his body in that position, or if the Lord did it, or if Louis laid himself out. I had turned my back for about thirty seconds to call my work to tell my boss I would not be in, and when I did not hear Louis laboring to breathe, I turned around to see him peacefully laid out on the bed and gone from this Earth. I do not know what happened in those thirty seconds, but I do know scripture says: "I give to them eternal life, and they shall never ever perish, and not anyone shall pluck them out of My hand" (John 10:28). The only hand that was there that moment was the hand of the Lord because Louis loved Jesus and He was in His hand.

I cannot really remember how I was feeling at this point. I just remember walking over to him, shaking him and asking if he was in there. When he did not respond, I remembering thinking, "Now what do I do?" He was gone, and I was left standing there without the husband that I had been with for twenty-four plus years. One of our daughters was down stairs sleeping, so the first thing I did was go down to wake her to tell her that her dad was dead. She immediately ran upstairs and checked her dad and told me that he was dead. She started dialing her sisters and brothers to tell them, and I just remember telling her not to let them know he was dead because I did not want to shock them. I told her to just have them come home.

One by one the children came home; each one reacting in different ways as they saw their father lying dead on his hospital bed. I tried very hard to make sure each one had the support they needed, but I was in so much shock I did not know what to do. My eldest son, John Jr., entered the room and took over. He started letting people have time alone with Louis and called any others that needed called. Many hours passed as person after person visited Louis and said their goodbyes. There was not going to be a body to view because of the type of burial that Louis had selected. He was going to be buried in the first green cemetery (everything biodegradable, including the body). His body would not be embalmed, but was to be put on ice during the waiting period in order that funeral arrangements could be made. He was to be given a burial that was similar to a Jewish one (he was of Jewish heritage). He was naked and wrapped in a biodegradable linen cloth, laid on a bamboo board, and lowered into the ground in a hole that was only three feet deep. When the coroner came to take him, his little dog began to lie on his body and mourn. Sometimes, animals are more faithful than humans when it comes to friendship. When Louis' body was put on the stretcher, his little dog began to growl and tried to keep the body. Louis used to play a game called "bear dog" with his little dog. He had a stuffed bear that they would play tug-of-war with and growl. That crazy little dog went and picked up that bear and started bouncing up and down toward Louis' dead body hoping to get a response. This scene was almost as heart wrenching as the children one by one trying to accept that their father was actually gone. As the days went by, planning was happening. My sister, Rae, came and she helped with the memorial service. Louis died on Good Friday, so it was Easter time and his favorite flower happened to be lilies. We ordered many of them and made a poster that was called the "seasons of life". We started in the spring (birth thru childhood) went to summer (young adulthood) went to autumn (mid-life) and then to winter (the Leukemia and the last year of his life). We found this appropriate because in the Word of God, the Lord speaks of a time for everything under heaven. Ecclesiastes 3:1-2 states, "To everything there is a season. A time for every purpose under heaven: A time to be born, and a time to die . . ." this was his time to go and be with the Lord. At the beginning of his journey through Leukemia the Lord had answered his prayers about what was to happen and shared this particular season with Louis. If you, the reader, recall in the previous paragraphs you read the scriptures the Lord gave to Louis and explained to him that it was his time to go home. In addition, you will also remember that the Lord had forewarned me that Louis was going to die and then part of the way through his walk through Leukemia the Lord shared with me why Louis had to leave this Earth. There were many reasons, but one of the main ones had to do with his job in heaven. The Lord has taken me to heaven a few times during my twenty-seven years of salvation, (of which I will share in the following chapters), and during one of my visits there Jesus explained that when a person dies and goes to heaven, there is a job waiting up there for him or her. I often think Christians think eternity is just spent worshipping and sitting at Jesus' feet or in such awe we don't know what to do. But in reality, we all have jobs to do up there. In heaven, there are those who are worshipping, there are those who do teaching (the 12 disciples are an example of this), there are those who do dance, there are those who are prayer warriors, those who are helping prepare for the final battle, and so forth. A few months before Louis passed away, the Lord shared with me that he was needed in heaven so that he could lead an intercessory prayer team that would be praying for those individuals who will become Christians during the final Tribulation. When I questioned the Lord on this, He shared with me that in

Hebrews 12:1 it states, "Therefore we also, since we are surrounded by so great a cloud of witnesses, let us lay aside every weight, and the sin which so easily ensnares us, and let us run with endurance the race that is set before us . . ." The "Great Cloud of Witnesses" are the saints that have gone before us, and one of the ways in which they surround us, and as scripture states, "cheer us on in our race set before us" is through prayer. Louis was going to be one of the saints gone before that would help with the prayer. Many times I wonder if we realize that God has us being Christ's "hands and feet" on the Earth and this will continue in Eternity. Jesus declares this when He stated in John 14:12, "Very truly I tell you, whoever believes in me will do the works I have been doing, and they will do even greater things than these, because I am going to the Father."

After the burial the months that lay ahead of us were filled with the twists and turns of grief. All the children became, what I saw as, "displaced." They all started searching for an identity, and ways in which they could cope. Sadly, the decisions made were not always the best. Before Louis died, he wrote letters to each child and in a time-crunch desperation tried to repair damage he had caused during the last few years of his life. It was told to me later by one his

Oncologists, that he probably had Leukemia for quite a while in his life and this could have very well started to affect his mind so that he experienced the Dementia type symptoms because the oxygen level in his blood was compromised. Because of these types of symptoms, his behavior was anything but predictable. The rages that happened affected all in the house and the verbal abuse became unbearable. As he became more unpredictable, the trust level dropped and so we all stared pulling away emotionally. This was a very strange and difficult place to find oneself after a death.

Michaela, who was always seen as his first born princess, was lost without her father. She ended up moving 1600 miles away and searching for her life. What she has found is two and a half years of sadness and different destructive avenues to medicate the pain. She stopped believing in God, and continues to search for her way. Grace actually grieved pretty well, and got married to the man she had been dating and had a child after a few months. She does not attend a church because of the betrayal of various pastors over the years and the final betrayal of the Christian counselor. Faye also moved 1600 miles away to search for the answers to fill the void of no father. She struggled because she felt that her father had always bought her obedience by giving her small gifts to make her behave. Later she felt that her father did not want any relationship with her. This caused her to search for someone to accept her, and has experienced much heartache from a man she has been in relationship with. Seth had a very odd and quirky, yet strained, relationship with his father, so he regressed back into behaving like a very young teenager. Seth never seemed to shed tears of grief. Seth stated, "If tears were there, I would let them come, but they aren't because I am comforted to know my dad is in heaven." Even so, for a very long time, there was an existence of living in a fantasy world of video games (played with his best friend) and books. Our youngest daughter showed very little emotion, and her world became a secret place that no one could really enter into. Her emotions went from one extreme to the next as she struggled to find her way through grief. The next year became a time where our family drew closer together emotionally, yet further apart physically. As I stated before, three of my girls now lived in another state, three of my children lived in the house with me, and John Jr. moved to another state. I felt as if my family unit was fragmented and pieces were scattered everywhere, yet God was putting the pieces of the puzzle into place.

At this point, almost three years have passed and each one is starting to move into adulthood and their places in life. Some are good, and some are not so good.

Months passed as grief and sadness started to be replaced by acceptance and small pieces of joy and happiness. It seemed very strange to have Louis gone. When the hospital bed and all the equipment was removed, it became very apparent he was gone from this Earth forever.

Back tracking a bit, I will share the events of the funeral so that you, the reader, can become a part of the celebration of Louis' life. Funerals often become a sad and oppressive event, but when one thinks of what has really happened, one will realize that it is a celebration of a believer getting to go home to the Lord. Before Louis died, he requested a few things. One was that a very dear friend of ours, Diane, and I would dance a tambourine dance at his funeral and then play a very rock and roll version of a song called "There Ain't No Grave." Louis' favorite Jewish song was "Baruch Adonai" and had a tremendous beat to it, so Diane and I danced this and then she did a dance to the latter song with "wings" (a form of a worship instrument). Our youngest daughter started the service with the blowing of the shofar to symbolize that Louis had gone home to be with Jesus and then our five daughters sang the song, "How Great Thou Art" which was another of Louis' favorite songs; the harmony was beautiful and amazing. The dances were the next in line and then we had a time where people could come up and share funny, happy, strange, or amazing stories about Louis and the events of his life. Each of his children and I shared first, and then the microphone was opened to all his friends, co-workers, and whoever else felt inclined to share.

The day was bitter cold and rainy, so when we all went to the burial site things went quite quickly. There was a quick prayer, song, and flowers thrown into a three-foot hole where Louis' body was then laid. Everyone returned for a dinner and fellowship time. It was very tiring and quite emotional and all were exhausted. As the days moved forward, grief and sorrow became me and the children's closest friends. Days turned into weeks, weeks into months and grief and numbness seemed forever looming. Eight months after Louis' death, Faye and Michaela both decided to move out and go to a different state. That added to the sorrow. I felt as if my family was fragmented and quickly scattering like dandelion seeds in the wind. Grace got married and had a son and they moved into my house, Seth, my youngest son, continued in school and got a decent job and he stayed in my house. Our youngest daughter plugged away at school and being a young, single mom and she also stayed in the house. There were an incredible amount of people living in one house; I was overwhelmed, and I found myself fighting incredible anger. I could not even get to sadness or grief; I seemed to constantly be angry at Louis. Also, during this time, I was attending to the counselor molestation incident and this became the greatest trial I had ever faced.

During the first few months after Louis' death, the Lord decided to take me to heaven three more times. He had already taken me twice during my walk with Him. Each time, He sent me back with messages for the Church body. I will be relaying all these visits and messages in a following chapter. But right now, I will share with you, the reader, the rest of the grief journey.

By June, my heart had become very angry toward Louis. I felt as if he had robbed me of many years of my life because of the craziness and abuse to me and the children. I found myself crying to the hospice grief counselor explaining my dilemma. I told her that I felt tremendous guilt for being angry at Louis, and I felt ashamed that I could not be sad. In fact, I found myself glad that he was gone because now the craziness of life could stop, and I could hopefully live a normal life. She explained to me that it was not uncommon for women who lived in abuse to feel such a way when their spouse died. After listening to me gush all the grief, guilt, shame, and so forth, she made a statement to me that started my path to healing and being able to grieve. She told me that maybe I could think of Louis' death as a "gift" to me and that this could possibly relieve some of the guilt. After she hung up, she was absolutely correct, the guilt and shame started to depart when I thought about the gift I was given. I actually started to feel sad about Louis dying and was able to see the good parts about him and our life that was left in my memory. Sometimes God uses an individual to spark the beginning of a healing. This is what happened here. Her words were a "spring board" for God to soften my heart in order to finish the healing; this healing was not just my feelings about Louis, but also about churches and pastors.

I found myself not attending a formal "church" after Louis' death for about a year. I would just watch sermons at home, and then one morning when I awoke the Lord impressed upon me to go back to the church we were attending when Jean died. I was still scared, but I knew that I trusted this Pastor and his wife. When we left that church, it was only to start a ministry at a different church. We left under blessing, and so I felt as if it was "safe" to return. You see at this point, we had been in numerous churches rising up ministries and it seemed as soon as we became leaders, the darkness (demonic forces) would rush in and start using Christians to speak and act in very non-Christian ways. We would find the Lord intervening to protect us, and we would be directed to hand over the current ministry, quietly move on to another church to rise up another ministry. So, as to not get off on a "bunny trail," I started regularly attending this church. The trials were still happening with our youngest daughter and her situation, so in the next three to six months, I went to the church but stayed very reserved. Also, I was dealing with a lot of health issues. I developed fibromyalgia, and was dealing with a lot of migraine headaches that started leaving me dizzy all the time (twenty-four hours a day, seven days a week). My work life started suffering because of this. I had seen a lot of doctors and started going to the National Dizzy and Balance center to try and control all of this stuff. Much of it happened because of the extreme stress I had experienced over the years. After the six month period of time attending the church, the Lord impressed on me to go up to the altar, get anointed with oil, and receive healing prayer from some of the elders. In the scriptures it states, "Is anyone among you sick? Let them call the elders of the church to pray over them and anoint them with oil in the name of the Lord. And the prayer offered in faith will make the sick person well; the Lord will raise them up. If they have sinned, they will be forgiven" (James 5:14-15). I knew the Lord had impressed this upon my heart, so I was assuming that He was going to heal me. That is exactly what happened. It was not an instantaneous healing, it happened gradually over the next few hours. In fact, when I left the church there really was no change. Then suddenly, as I was driving, the Lord whispered to me, "Lily, are you dizzy?" I was not!!!! I couldn't believe it. When I got home, the Lord impressed upon me to stand in the corner and turn my head. I could actually do it without falling over. This was something I could not do before. He told me walk up and down the stairs. Before now, I would have to hold the railing and take one small step at a time for fear of falling over because I was so dizzy. In fact, for some odd reason the night before I had told my son-in-law to watch how difficult it was to climb the stairs. In addition, I showed him that I could not even stand without holding a wall. He was astounded that I could normally walk the stairs; in fact I could quickly go up and down without a rail. He was astounded at the miracle, as was I. My sister then called and asked me to attend a movie at the theatre which I could not have done before because it made me so incredibly dizzy, and when I got there I was astounded at what I could do. I told her to watch me; I proceeded to walk like I was on a balance beam and was not dizzy. She, her daughter, and I just stood praising the Lord for the miracle He had done. The next Sunday I testified at the church of the great miracle the Lord had done. After the testimony, the Lord spoke to my heart and told me to go back up to the missionary and ask the wife if she would pray for me for emotional healing for what the counselor had done to my daughter and give me the ability to deal with and let go of every negative emotion. We ended up meeting for two sessions of deep inner healing. God not only healed my emotions from what the counselor had done, but also from any residue of the damage from Louis and any residual anger I held against him. From that day forward, the Fibromyalgia hurt less and the migraines became less. Praise the Lord!!! Sometimes, sickness can result from unforgiveness, bitterness, anger, or un-repented sins. Other times sickness can result from demonic oppression. In the Bible, Jesus healed many individuals just by telling them that their sins were forgiven and the individual would walk away healed. "Then a paralytic was brought to Him, carried by four men. Since they were unable to get to Jesus through the crowd, they uncovered the roof above Him, made an opening, and lowered the paralytic on his mat. When Jesus saw their faith, He said to the paralytic, "Son, your sins are forgiven."…Which is easier, to say to the paralytic, 'Your sins are forgiven'; or to say, 'Get up, and pick up your pallet and walk'? But so that you may know that the Son of Man has authority on earth to forgive sins'—He said to the paralytic, 'I say to you, get up, pick up your pallet and go home.' And he got up and immediately picked up the pallet and went out in the sight of everyone, so that they were all amazed and were glorifying God, saying, 'We have never seen anything like this.'" (Mark 2:3-5, 9-11). An example of sickness that is brought on by demonic oppression is in the story of the lady who was stooped over for years: "One Sabbath Jesus was teaching in one of the synagogues, and a woman there had been disabled by a spirit for eighteen years. She was hunched over and could not stand up straight. When Jesus saw her, He called her over and said, 'Woman, you are set free from your infirmity'"… (Luke 13:8-12).

After all this, the Lord was ready to bring me through to a new season of my life. He is in the process of doing so. I am walking in a season of incredible joy, blessing, favor, grace, and mercy. He has brought into my life new relationships, a career move with a promotion, renewed strength to my body, renewed joy in my heart, refreshing of my weary soul, and finally an increased move of the Holy Spirit in my life. Truly He has kept every promise from "**... Never** be afraid or discouraged, for the LORD God, **... He will** not **leave you** or abandon **you ...** God, even my God, **will** be with **you**; **he will** not fail **...** (1 Chronicles 28:20) " **...** Weeping may tarry for the night, but **joy comes** with the **morning. ...** (Psalm 30:5). I could quote many, many more of the promises that were fulfilled in my life through these trials but these are just two examples. Now, as promised, a short excerpt of the trial of child molestation.

# CHAPTER IX

## HURRICANE CHRISTIAN COUNSELOR:
## BETRAYAL OF AUTHORITY & BROKEN TRUST

This chapter will be short and to the point. This event was very traumatic and not much detail will be added for the sake of caring for the reputation and emotional health of all those involved. This event lasted over the course of approximately two years, from when our daughter was about fourteen years old until sixteen years old. It began when our daughter started to experience emotional trauma because of the way her father treated her, and I'm sure there were various other reasons if one was to ask her. Her father treated her far harsher than the other children and in addition, he verbally was not kind, to put it mildly. Because of this, as I see it, she was searching for a father figure. We ended up getting her help from a recovery center where she spent a few months. After getting out, I started letting her go to a Christian counselor. By this time her father had spiraled downhill and had minimal involvement in this process. During the next two years, the counselor started to become inappropriate in his behavior. Without our knowledge, he started seeing her outside appointed times, started secretly visiting and picking her up from her job, and started calling and texting her numerous times a month (approximately 1500 times in one month). Some days these calls and text would start at 3 a.m. and go straight through until 12:00 a.m. (midnight). Literally, there would be fifty to seventy calls and texts a day. I found this out by looking at the call logs. When the counselor discovered we had found out about the calls, he secretly bought track phones and got our daughters friends to give them to her. He was telling her that he loved her, wanted to marry her, and so forth. Eventually, he convinced her to be intimate with him. He also started to warp the Word of God and tell her lies about the Word of God (i.e. because of the forgiveness of the blood of Jesus, he was forgiven and was not sinning). He also convinced her that grace was extended even in these circumstances. Our daughter eventually started loving this man, in whatever capacity, it was real to her. This man was thirty-five plus years old and married with children.  He started lying to his wife when she started to suspect this behavior.

    When I started to suspect things were wrong, I called him and confronted him.  He lied to me and denied ever doing any of this.  I told him he could not see her anymore, but then he just started to sneak and lie more.  She was starting to get depressed, angry, and quit doing her school work and her grades began to drop.  As this was happening, others started to suspect there was wrong doing and began to come to me concerned.  It was then I decided to have a meeting with him to again ask him if he was being intimate with our daughter.  He denied it completely and made up stories of how he would NEVER do such a thing because he was a man of God.  He claimed this would be against the Word of God and boasted that he was married with children and would never do this.  I believed him; my mind could not comprehend that any godly man would do this to a child.  As her behavior and emotional state became more unstable and more and more people came to me and told me stories of what they were seeing, I had another meeting with the counselor where he again denied ever doing anything more than counselor her.  Again, I believed him until a very strange event happened.

My car had broken down, and I had to buy another one. When this happened, one of our daughters told my husband and me not to buy another car because a tragedy that would be the worst thing we had ever experienced was coming. I could not understand this. I actually told my husband that I could not comprehend any tragedy greater than the death of our daughter and grandson which was already experienced. We ended up buying the car.

Upon the arrival home, we were met with the news that our daughter was now pregnant. She was scheduled to go away for ten days. We let her go, but while she was gone we found out much more than we ever wanted to know as parents. When she arrived back home from her trip, the tragic story unfolded. Needless to say, we ended up meeting with the counselor only to find out he was the father to the child, his wife and family were in great crisis because of this, the church where he belonged was falling to pieces, and many lies and deception were going on (inclusive of the fact that he had called child protection and made false accusations against me, only for them to find out he had lied to try and get my daughter from me, with intent to have her for himself). In the meeting, he even had the audacity to use scripture to tell us that we were not allowed to be angry because God would only want us to forgive and then proceeded to use scripture to tell us we could not involve the law because Christians were only to use the church for legal matters. Emotions were raging, and the mistrust, lies, deception, and betrayal was beyond what I could endure. I broke into tears; my husband and I left the meeting telling him to NEVER contact our family or daughter again.

    Police were called and investigations started. Restraint orders and Domestic No Contact Orders placed, yet the man kept coming back over and over disregarding even the law. On top of all this, he called my other daughters to tell them they had no right to be angry because as Christians it was their job to just forgive him. Days turned into months as the investigators uncovered more and more secrets. There ended up being more young girls and even children that he had done this to. He ended up having an internet site where he was sending child pornography out to young girls. When all was said and done, he was ordered into sex therapy where he was kicked out because he was so "far gone".

    During this, Louis fought the Leukemia battle, I continued to try to hold a family together, work a job, take care of a sick husband, nurture a failing marriage, and mother an angry and emotional pregnant teen. Psalm 91 and Psalm 46 became my constant companions. The Lord became my strong tower, my refuge, a shadow of wings where I could be protected, my saving grace, all mercy, joy of my salvation, calm in the storm, and all knowing guide and wisdom. He became the only place of solitude and comfort. He gave the grace to walk this impossible walk. The baby was born and soon after Louis passed away; Louis was struggling to die and leave me with this mess, but by the grace of God, I was able to comfort him and assure him that the Lord would take care of me and the children. A few months after Louis death, I was dealing with incredible anger toward this counselor. I was finding myself going to county attorney meetings and having to deal with all sorts of lies and deceptions. Each week finding out more disgusting and horrible things he had done over the course of eighteen years (his entire adulthood). Finally, the day came to go to the court room and see him sentenced. He had plea bargained and was getting a very slim sentence instead of the maximum sentence which he should have received (in my opinion). I wrote up the report that I was to deliver to the court which contained all the ways in which he had hurt each member of my family. When I was done speaking, the counselor was allowed to talk. He gave quite the speech, and one statement he made was that he would spend the rest of his life trying to make better what he had done. Funny thing, the night before, he told the investigator that I was putting him in prison, and he hated me. Also, said it was my entire fault that he was in this predicament. The judge addressed him by telling him that his acts were vile and he could never fix what he had done to my family. Then the judge went on to tell him that he had set his own sentence out of his mouth and that he would spend the rest of his life as a registered child pedophile. The judge gave him the maximum sentence he was allowed to give by law and it was over. The counselor was taken away to prison where he is still serving time.

    Through this trial, God taught me so much. I prayed for his family the entire time, even though there were things his wife did that complicated this process. She is standing by him and waiting for his prison term to be finished. She told me in a meeting, she believed the Lord wanted her to stay and stand beside her husband. I pray for her strength and endurance during this time. I pray that their children do not suffer too much from this circumstance. But one incredible "God" thing happened the night before the trial. To be honest, there were many times I prayed that God would let the counselor die. I was so miserable inside because my family was shattered: sibling relationships were very strained or completely destroyed, my relationship with my daughter was completely gone because she blamed me for everything that happened to him, and stress and sickness hit each member of my family in a different way. I was burning with anger and unforgiveness. Finally, came the night of brokenness and healing for me, ironically enough, it was the night before the court trial where the counselor was being sentenced. My sister had asked me if I would go to a conference with her. At this conference, the holy man of God came out and his sermon was about forgiveness and how one drop of the blood of Jesus has the power to forgive and heal any sin. He started with a statement, "Think about the worse sin anyone has ever committed against you; now know that one drop of the blood of Jesus has the power to forgive that sin." He went on to talk about how all sin is seen the same and each sin had to be forgiven on the cross. The Word of God states, ". . . You have come to **Jesus**, the one who mediates the new covenant between God and people, and to the sprinkled **blood**, which speaks of **forgiveness …"** (Hebrews 12:24). He stated that if Christ could forgive your sin, then one can forgive even the worse sin ever committed against them. I broke down in a heap of tears and was able to forgive the counselor, I was even able to pray for his salvation and asked the Lord to send a minister to the prison and help save, deliver, and heal him and his family. I asked the Lord to forgive me for my thoughts of malice, anger, bitterness, and unforgiveness for him. I walked away healed and any residue left was removed at the church a few months ago when I had deep emotional healing prayer and Jesus completed the work. As the Lord has promised in his Word, "and I am certain that God, who began the good work within you, will continue his work until it is finally finished on the day when Christ Jesus returns." (Philippians 1:6). God is still restoring my family piece by piece, bit by bit, but this much I know, He will continue until His promise of household salvation and restoration is finished and perfected. He has even taken this horrible event that the devil hoped would destroy my family and brought good out of it. Genesis 50:19-20 states, "but Joseph said to them, "Don't be afraid. Am I in the place of God? You intended to harm me, but God intended it for good to accomplish what is now being done, the saving of many lives." Relationships are close and doing well between some of the siblings and in Jesus' name the rest will come around. Strength, beauty, and joy have come to my family that was once shattered and broken. He has brought new relationships, beautiful grandchildren, and a strength that could not have come without this trial. Summing up this chapter, I will leave you with this thought, God is able to take all of your pain, grief, sorrow, trials, tribulations, sickness, debt, loneliness, depression, and anything else that holds you bound and provide a way for you. I will leave you with this thought, The Word of God states this, He will "provide for those who grieve in Zion-- to bestow on them a crown of beauty instead of ashes, the oil of joy instead of mourning, and a garment of praise instead of a spirit of despair. They will be called oaks of righteousness, a planting of the LORD for the display of his splendor" (Isaiah 61:3).

The final chapter you will read contains messages from the throne room of heaven. The Lord states, ". . . From everyone who has been given much, much will be demanded; and from the one who has been entrusted with much, much more will be asked." This may seem an odd verse to quote at this time, but I believe God has allowed many trials, but through this has given much grace, mercy, love, compassion, strength, and so forth. He has also seen in His infinite wisdom to trust me with heavenly messages and has required the writing of this book to relay these messages.

# CHAPTER X

# ANGELS PRESENT & HEAVENLY ENCOUNTERS

Where does one begin when God has so seen fit to take one into heaven and show secrets from the throne, and then entrust one to bring back messages. I will do my best to relay these messages in the best fashion I know how.

Each time I was taken up, angels appeared and escorted me to the throne informing me that I had a divine appointment with Christ. Each time a new message was sent back. The first time I went to heaven was about fifteen years ago. I had been on a forty day fast and at the end a woman prophesied to me and told me five angels would visit me. A few days later during a worship service five angels appeared and took me to heaven. I was suspended above the throne of Jesus Christ and was allowed to watch a worship service. It was astounding and breath-taking. The song, *Majesty,* was playing in the service where I was worshipping. Amazing thing was that in heaven the same song was coming up, as well as thousands of other ones. I was told by the angels that when worship happens on Earth, heaven partakes, even if there are vast songs happening. I'm not sure how to explain this, but it was not chaos, but beauty. All I know was that I saw millions of people worshipping at the throne, as far as the eye could see there were people. Angels were present flying around, and the twelve elders were there. When the chorus of the song played, they all would take their crowns and drop them at the feet of Jesus and they would all go face down. Then when verses were sung, they would pick up the crowns again. All in unison and all amazing as the music was sung and played in perfect harmony and tone. Then the angels all opened up their wings and flew in a circle around the top of the throne. An awesome crown was spinning above Jesus' head and when the chorus came, the throne would rise up and Jesus' head would meet the crown. When the song was over, I was back down in the church service. The message sent: Praise and worship in heaven enthrones King Jesus, and lifts Him high. Glory and strength comes out of the throne as this happens. This is confirmed in Psalm 22:3 when it states, "Yet you are holy, enthroned on the praises of Israel."

The second time was about ten years ago. I had taken a trip with my friend and sister; we prayed and worshipped for about thirty-six hours while driving. About twenty hours into the trip, an angel showed up and took me into heaven. My friend told me that my physical body actually left the car and an angel was driving in my place (I am still wow-ed by that one)!! While up in heaven, Jesus took my hand and walked me room to room. These rooms were full of worship items. Fabrics of garments that were more beautiful than anything Earth can provide; colors that were so bright, radiant, and beautiful and silks and satins that were so shiny yet iridescent at the same time. Tambourines were made of gold and silver and had glass "tinkles" on them that had a pure and holy sound. There were instruments that looked like a King's scepter with a prism on the end. They were used like batons, but when the light from Christ hit the prisms, rainbows filled heaven. Flags, banners, and streamers were all shapes and sizes with radiant colors and fabrics. I got to see these and touch them; Jesus showed me how to use each of them. Then I was taken over to watch worship happen with them, all of heaven partook. Interestingly enough, when dances took place there was no gravity, so the people could fly around the throne and could flip and spin in the air. Lots of children did this as they laughed and sang. Much more was seen and Jesus spoke of many things, but the message that was supposed to be given down here on Earth was that when one worships, it should be freely and without inhibition. Nothing should be held back, because God desires freedom and holiness in worship and praise. Three different places the Word talks of different worship positions, places, and heart conditions:

Psalms 29:2 states, "Ascribe to the LORD the glory due his name; worship the LORD in the splendor of holiness."

Psalms 95:6 states, "Oh come, let us worship and bow down; let us kneel before the LORD, our Maker!"

Psalms 99:5 states, "Exalt the LORD our God; worship at his footstool! Holy is he!"

Obviously, one can see that worshipping God is a command, yet a great honor that Christians have been given.

 The last three times were after Louis died. In my times of grief, sorrow, pain, and brokenness the Lord chose to take me up and shares great secrets. Each time I was shown different throne rooms in heaven where the Lord sits, stairways that are lit with purifying fire, beautiful veils that hang in front of thrones, crystal mountains with fiery thrones on top of them, fields of flowers, crystal seas, streets of gold, and streams that are so blue one can see through them. I watched different people who were doing their service for the King. There were intercessory groups, just like here on Earth, praise and worship groups, teachers teaching, children playing and laughing, mansions for as far as one can see, and so much more. One message that was sent with me was mentioned earlier in the book. The Lord told me to tell the church that a great cloud of witnesses is there spurring them on through prayer. Forever intercession is happening, not only from Jesus to God, but from those already in heaven. The other message was that when one gets to heaven, things are operated a lot like the church body here. Everyone has a job to do and all work in unity to glorify God. The most important message that came out of these three visits was the last message. Jesus walked me through a portion of a city. It was the most incredible sight I had ever seen. He shared with me that I was walking through part of the New Jerusalem. We were walking on a gold street, but the sight that awed me was the golden pillars that lined the streets. As far up as one could see and as far as one could look ahead these pillars extended. They were made of a gold that actually looked crystal. Engraved on them – spiraling upward were as many names as one could read. The scripture in revelation came into my mind. Revelation 3:12, "The one who is victorious I will make a pillar in the temple of my God. Never again will they leave it. I will write on them the name of my God and the name of the city of my God, the new Jerusalem, which is coming down out of heaven from my God; and I will also write on them my new name." Jesus then said to me, "Lily, go tell my Bride that it is true. There is a city that I am bringing down to the Earth and they are a part of the city. Their names are engraved on the pillars which are contained within the city. Some do not believe this to be true, but assure them that it is true!" By this time I was sobbing so hysterically that I could hardly stand. Even as I write this, my heart can hardly contain the message that so urgently came from the lips of Jesus Christ. My dear sisters and brothers in Christ, Jesus is on the horizon ready to burst forth the clouds to get His Bride – US!!! Are you ready? Is He your all in all? Does our King sit on the Throne of your heart? Have you allowed Him to free you, deliver you, transform you, but most importantly – LOVE YOU! If not, this moment I would encourage you to surrender your life and call unto the Lord, and He will hear you. He WILL come and sit on the throne of your heart. He will be your lover, best friend, King, provider, spouse, comforter, guide, healer, deliverer, forgiveness, teacher, wisdom - in general – God is your everything! He stated to Moses in Exodus 3:14 – **I AM WHO I AM!** I would say to you today, **HE IS** all you need.

## IT'S TRUE MY FRIEND:

"I saw the Holy City, the new Jerusalem, coming down out of heaven from God, prepared as a bride beautifully dressed for her husband" Revelation 21:2!

Made in the USA
Columbia, SC
14 July 2021